THE COURSE COMPANION
FOR
BHS STAGE ONE

THE COURSE COMPANION
FOR
BHS STAGE ONE

MAXINE CAVE

BHSSM+T

J. A. ALLEN
London

British Library Cataloguing-in-Publication Data.
A catalogue record for this book is available from the British Library.

ISBN 978-0-85131-765-6

Published in Great Britain in 2000 by
J. A. Allen
an imprint of Robert Hale Ltd
Clerkenwell House
45–47 Clerkenwell Green
London EC1R 0HT

www.halebooks.com

Typesetting and production: Bill Ireson
Colour photography: Bob Langrish
Illustrations: Maggie Raynor
Cover design: Nancy Lawrence
Colour separation by Tenon &Polert Colour Scanning Ltd
Printed in China by Midas Printing International Ltd

Contents

Introduction   *ix*

Plan for the BHS examinations   *x*

Points of the horse   *xi*

1   Points of the Horse and Identification   **1**
         Points of the Horse   1
         Equine Gender   1
         Height   1
         Markings   2
         Colours   5
         Follow-up Work to Confirm Knowledge and Experience   12
         Helpful Hints and Exam Technique   12

2   Handling Horses in Everyday Situations   **13**
         Catching a Horse from the Field   13
         Tying Up   15
         Handling   16
         Approaching a Horse   17
         Leading and "Standing Up"   18
         Turning Out   21
         Follow-up Work to Confirm Knowledge and Experience   22
         Helpful Hints and Exam Technique   22

3   Grooming   **24**
         Reasons for Grooming   24
         The Grooming Kit   24
         Some General Points   28
         Method   31
         Follow-up Work to Confirm Knowledge and Experience   32
         Helpful Hints and Exam Technique   33

4   **Bedding and the Mucking Out Procedure**   **35**
         Bedding Systems   35
         Types of Bedding   35
         Some General Points on Mucking Out   37
         Full Mucking Out Procedure for a Straw Bed   40
         Variations for Full Mucking Out of a Shavings Bed   41
         Building and Maintaining a Muck Heap   41
         Muck Heap Disposal   43
         Follow-up Work to Confirm Knowledge and Experience   43
         Helpful Hints and Exam Technique   44

5   **Horse Psychology**   **46**
         Natural Instincts and Lifestyle   46
         The Domesticated Horse in the Field   48
         Horses that are Difficult to Catch   51
         The Stabled Horse   52
         The Horse when Ridden   55
         Follow-up Work to Confirm Knowledge and Experience   58
         Helpful Hints and Exam Technique   58

6   **The Field-kept Horse and Grassland Management**   **60**
         Fencing   60
         Water   63
         Shelter   64
         Maintaining Good Pasture   64
         Daily Checks   66
         Follow-up Work to Confirm Knowledge and Experience   67
         Helpful Hints and Exam Technique   67

7   **Feeding**   **68**
         The Rules of Feeding and Watering   68
         Types of Feed   70
         Deciding What to Feed   73
         Follow-up Work to Confirm Knowledge and Experience   78
         Helpful Hints and Exam Technique   78

8   **Saddlery, Its Use, Care and Fitting**   **80**
         Tacking up Procedure   80
         Fitting the Equipment   84

	Care of the Equipment	87
	Injuries from Dirty or Ill-fitting Tack	89
	Follow-up Work to Confirm Knowledge and Experience	91
	Helpful Hints and Exam Technique	91
9	**Horse Clothing**	**92**
	Rugs	92
	Tail Bandages	99
	Follow-up Work to Confirm Knowledge and Experience	102
	Helpful Hints and Exam Technique	102
10	**Shoeing**	**103**
	The External Structure of the Foot	103
	Recognising the Need for Reshoeing	103
	Follow-up Work to Confirm Knowledge and Experience	106
	Helpful Hints and Exam Technique	108
11	**Health**	**109**
	Signs of the Horse being in Good Health	109
	Signs of the Horse being Unwell	111
	Follow-up Work to Confirm Knowledge and Experience	112
	Helpful Hints and Exam Technique	112
12	**Safety When Working and Riding**	**113**
	Safety	113
	Accident Procedure and Reports	118
	Knowledge of the BHS	121
	Follow-up Work to Confirm Knowledge and Experience	121
	Helpful Hints and Exam Technique	122
13	**Preparing to Take the Exam**	**123**
	Location	123
	Clothing	123
	Performance	126
	Index	*127*

Introduction

This book covers the horse care and knowledge elements of the British Horse Society Stage One examination, along with some subject matter which leads on to the BHS Stage Two.

Each chapter has headings and divisions which make it easier for the student to cover all aspects of the syllabus. However, it is still very important that each student studies the contents of the BHS syllabus before taking any exam. If students intend to go on beyond Stage One they should realise that at each new level they should have confirmed and improved their knowledge from the level before. For example, grooming is examined at Stage One, but will be looked at again at Stage Two.

The practical skills outlined within the book must be developed through "hands on" experience. There is no substitute for practical work.

In the section "Helpful Hints and Exam Technique" I have tried to highlight areas where, as an examiner, I frequently find candidates in trouble through misinformation, lack of preparation or misunderstanding of the requirements of the examination situation.

Maxine Cave

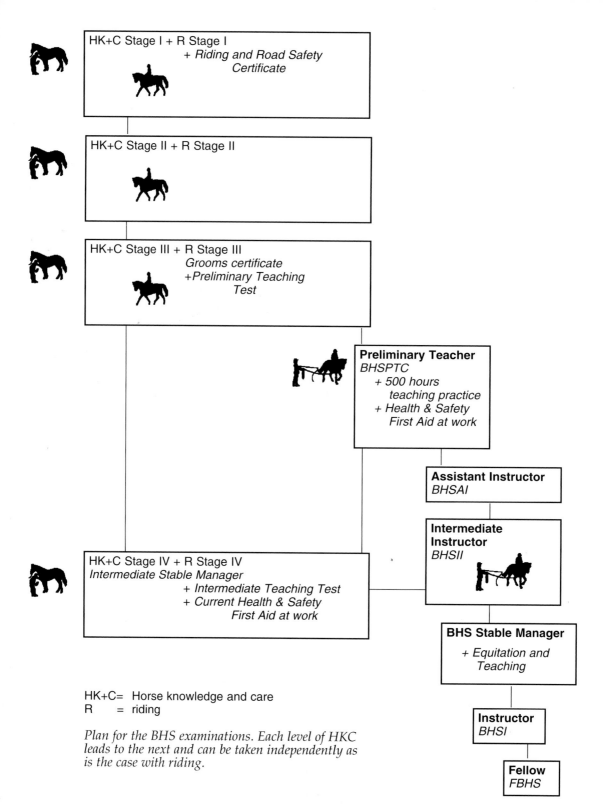

HK+C Stage I + R Stage I
+ *Riding and Road Safety
Certificate*

HK+C Stage II + R Stage II

HK+C Stage III + R Stage III
*Grooms certificate
+Preliminary Teaching
Test*

Preliminary Teacher
BHSPTC
*+ 500 hours
teaching practice
+ Health & Safety
First Aid at work*

Assistant Instructor
BHSAI

**Intermediate
Instructor**
BHSII

HK+C Stage IV + R Stage IV
*Intermediate Stable Manager
+ Intermediate Teaching Test
+ Current Health & Safety
First Aid at work*

BHS Stable Manager
*+ Equitation and
Teaching*

Instructor
BHSI

Fellow
FBHS

HK+C= Horse knowledge and care
R   = riding

*Plan for the BHS examinations. Each level of HKC
leads to the next and can be taken independently as
is the case with riding.*

Forehand   Middle   Hindquarters

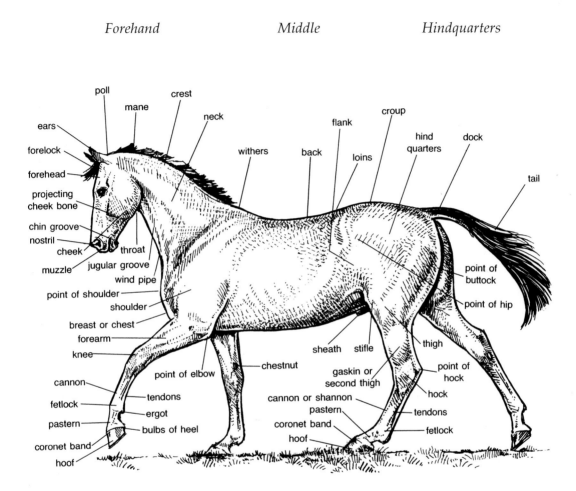

poll

crest

mane

neck

flank   croup

ears

withers   back   loins

hind
quarters   dock

forelock

forehead

tail

projecting
cheek bone

chin groove

nostril

cheek   throat

muzzle   jugular groove

wind pipe

point of shoulder

shoulder

breast or chest

forearm

knee

point of elbow   chestnut

sheath   stifle   thigh

point of
buttock

point of hip

cannon

tendons

gaskin or
second thigh

point of
hock

fetlock

ergot

cannon or shannon   hock

pastern

bulbs of heel

pastern

coronet band

tendons

coronet band

hoof   fetlock

hoof

Points of the horse

1 Points of the Horse and Identification

1. Points of the Horse

Learning the points of the horse is an essential aid to describing the horse and communicating with each other. For example, if you needed to describe to a vet, over the telephone, where your horse had been wounded, you can then give him or her an accurate picture of the problem.

2. Equine Gender

a. Filly – This term is usually applied to a female horse until she is fully grown.
b. Mare – A fully grown female horse.
c. Colt – This term is usually applied to a male horse until he is full grown or gelded.
d. Stallion – A fully grown male horse that has not been gelded (i.e. "entire").
e. Gelding – A male horse that has been castrated (the testes are removed) so that it cannot reproduce. Most male horses are gelded as this makes them easier to handle.
f. Rig – This is a male horse with either one or both testes retained in the abdomen (undescended).

3. Height

Horses are measured in hands. Their height is always expressed in hands and inches; for example, 15.2 h.h. (the "h.h." stands for "hands high"). One hand equals 4 in (approximately 10 cm). The measurement is taken

Measuring the horse's height

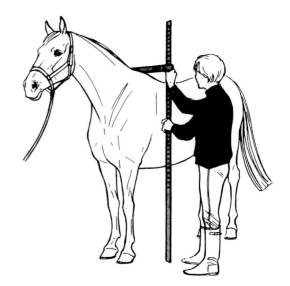

from the ground to the highest point of the horse's withers. For accurate measurement, the horse should be asked to stand square, unshod, on level ground. If students know their own height in hands, it can help them to estimate the height of a horse. As the horse may be suspicious of the measuring stick, it should be untied and held by an assistant while it is being measured, in order to prevent it from panicking and pulling back.

4. Markings

a. White or striped hooves – These are usually accompanied by white leg markings.

b. White socks – Front or hind limbs that are white from the coronet upwards, with any variation in height as far as the knee or hock.

c. White stockings – The same as white socks but describing any variation in height over and above the knee and hock.

d. White coronet – If the white marking is so small that it hardly extends beyond the coronet, it would be misleading to call it a sock. In this situation it is called a white coronet.

e. Ermine marks – These are black dots on a white sock. They usually only appear around the coronet and pastern.

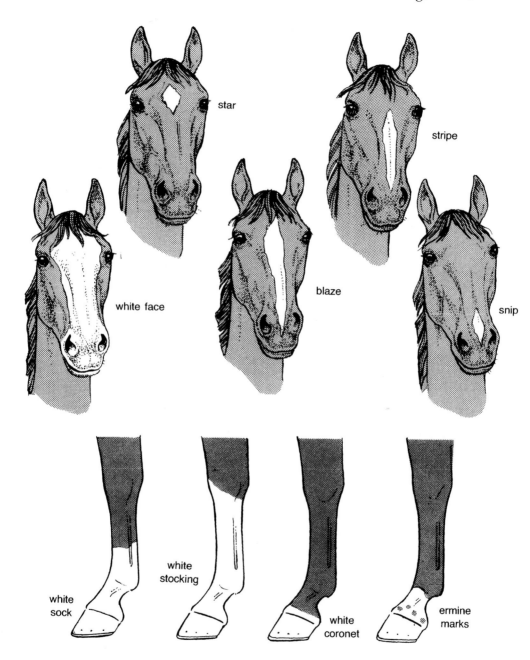

Face and leg markings

f.   Star – A white mark in the middle of the forehead. It may be very small. If it covers a very wide area, it would be called a white forehead.

g.   Blaze – A large white patch on the forehead, extending down the middle of the face as a broad stripe, usually finishing at or near the end of the upper lip.

h.   Stripe – A white line, too narrow to be called a blaze but extending down the face in the same way.

- Learning the points of the horse is an essential aid to describing the horse and in communicating with other people, especially if there are specific problems – for example, explanations to the vet.

i.   White nostril/lip, etc. – The best way to describe a small white marking anywhere around the muzzle. Also called a "snip". Snips can also be flesh- coloured.

j.   White face – Sometimes a blaze extends over such a wide area that it is better described in this way.

k.   White markings are often found in other areas as a result of scarring. They are common around the withers, from old saddle sores. These should simply be described according to what you see. For example: "two small white marks on the nearside of the withers".

l.   Black points – Horses with black stockings, a black mane and tail, black tips to the ears and a black muzzle are said to have black points.

m. Dorsal or eel stripe – This is a long black stripe on the back, which extends from the withers along the line of the spine to the top of the tail. It is common in the dun-coloured horse.

n.   Mealy muzzle – This is a light, biscuit-brown colouring covering the muzzle.

o.   Flaxen mane and tail – Some horses (mostly chestnuts) have manes and tails of a creamy-yellow colour, termed flaxen.

p.   Whorls – These are areas where hair grows out in different directions from one point. They are individual to each horse, just as fingerprints are individual to humans. Whorls are often rosette-shaped. Those that extend upwards/sideways are termed "feathered".

q. Dapples – These look like a series of circles incorporated into the horse's colouring. Most common in the dapple grey, but many bays are also dappled.

5. Colours

a. Bay – The body colouring of the horse is brown. The mane and tail must be black. The bay may have socks or stockings and various face markings. They often have black points and may have a mealy muzzle. There are many different shades of bay – mahogany bay, bright bay, dark bay, light bay, etc. Bays have dark skin and are the most likely colour to have ermine marks.

b. Chestnut – A yellow/ginger/brown colour, varying from light to dark, with mane and tail a similar colouring to the body or flaxen. (The mane and tail cannot be black, as the horse would then be a bay.) Chestnuts can have any combination of socks, stockings and face marking. Many chestnuts have pale, sensitive skin. A darker brown, without the yellow tint, is called a liver chestnut.

c. Grey – Generally quite dark in colouring as youngsters, greys gradually turn whiter. Their skin is dark and the coat contains a mixture of black, grey and white hairs. Very dark greys are called iron grey, those with circle-like patterns in their coats are called dapple grey and those with a freckled appearance are called flea-bitten grey.

d. Roan – A dark-skinned horse with white hairs mixed evenly into the main coat colouring. The black mane and tail also contain a mixture of white hairs. Shades of roan: strawberry, blue, grey, bay, red.

e. Piebald – The coat consists of patches of black hair and patches of white. The pattern of these

- To become expert at describing horses' colours and markings it is necessary to be observant and to look at as many horses and ponies as possible

Piebald

patches will vary tremendously. The mane and tail will usually be coloured according to the colour of the coat at their base of growth. For example, if the horse has black hair partway down its neck and then white hair, the mane will, correspondingly, be black partway and then white. The horse's skin will be dark under the black hair and pink under the white hair.

f. Skewbald – As for piebald, but with brown and white or any other colour patches. Both skewbald and piebald are often referred to as "coloured" horses.

g. Black – The coat, mane and tail must definitely be black, with no traces of brown hair. Any combination of white leg and face markings is acceptable.

h. Dun – The skin is dark but the main body of the coat is a pale biscuit-coloured brown. Duns have black points and a dorsal

Appaloosa

stripe. As with all colourings there are different shades. If the coat is more creamy than brown in colour, it is called yellow dun.

i. Cream – The skin is pale and the coat, mane and tail are all a creamy-white colour. It is sometimes possible to distinguish white leg and face markings on this cream coat.

j. Brown – The skin is dark and the coat, mane and tail are evenly dark brown. A brown horse is similar to a bay but does not have black points.

k. Appaloosa – A dark-skinned horse with a spotted coat. The coat is usually predominantly grey, with brown or black spots. There is an Appaloosa Society which lays down rules as to colouring.

l. Palomino – This colouring is like a very pale chestnut but not as pale as a cream, with flaxen mane and tail. The Palomino Society lays down specific regulations as to permitted colouring.

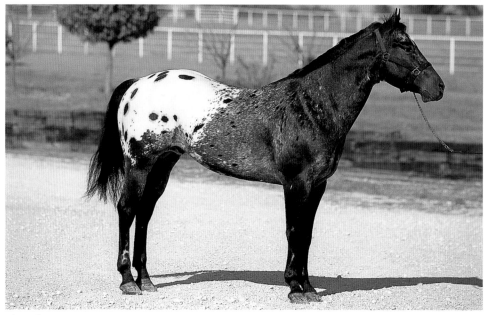

Appaloosa

Liver chestnut

Dapple grey

Palomino

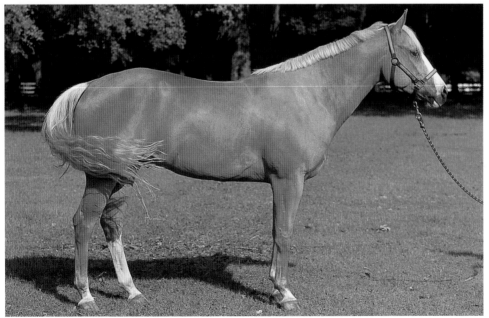

Piebald

Dun

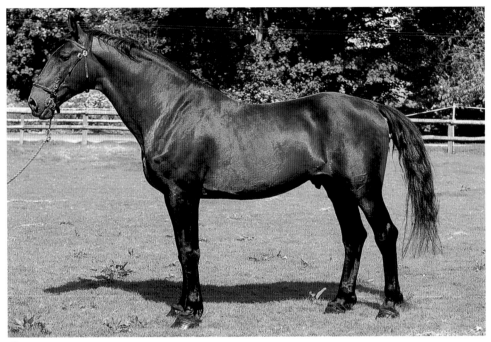

Bay

Skewbald

Follow-up Work to Confirm Knowledge and Experience

1. To become expert at describing horses' colours and markings it is necessary to be observant and to look at as many horses and ponies as possible. Going to shows, where many different horses are to be seen, provides an excellent opportunity for observing all sorts of colours and markings.
2. Measuring as many different horses as possible helps to develop a good eye for height.
3. Practise putting all the above information together to describe a horse. For example, "A 14.2 h.h. bay gelding. Black points, except for a white sock on the near hind. White star and white stripe tapering towards the nearside nostril", etc.

Helpful Hints and Exam Technique

Having learnt the points of the horse, make sure you can identify each point on a real horse. Looking at a picture in a book is never the same as when you have a three-dimensional horse in front of you. Try asking someone to call out all the points of the horse, in a random order, while you point them out on the horse.

When moving around the horse or pointing out any points of the horse, take care to show an understanding of safe procedure. If identifying a point on the hind limbs, make sure you still approach the horse at its shoulder and allow it to identify you. Then keep a hand in contact with the horse, stroking your way to the area in question. Never just dive in and prod the horse as you could be kicked.

2 Handling Horses in Everyday Situations

Students should be aware of safety when handling horses. The following basic methods of handling horses in fields and stables are essential steps towards safety for themselves and the horses.

1. Catching a Horse from the Field

a. If the horse is likely to be difficult to catch, take a reward, like a carrot or some pony cubes, in your pocket. If there are several horses in the field, they may gather around you expecting feed. You could find yourself caught in the middle of biting and kicking as these horses chase each other away. This is why it is not advisable to take a bucket into the field, as it will immediately attract the attention of all the horses.

b. Make sure you have a suitably sized head collar with a strong rope, and wear gloves to protect your hands while leading. If the horse is young or apt to be difficult, also wear a hard hat.

c. Enter the field and close the gate securely behind you.

d. Approach the horse quietly, walking towards its shoulder, with the head collar concealed behind your back if the horse is likely to be difficult. Remember that the horse has a blind spot immediately behind and in front of it. If you approach in this blind spot, you will startle it. If the horse does not appear to have seen you, announce your approach by calling its name. This may also encourage the horse to come towards you, which is preferable to you walking a long way into the field. There is less chance of having problems with other horses or the horse you are leading if you are only a short distance from the gate.

e. Allow the horse to smell you. Stroke its neck, then slip the rope over its neck to secure an initial hold on it.

f.   Standing close into its neck, facing forward, put on the head collar. In this way the horse can see what you are doing and you can move back with the horse if it steps backwards. If you stand in front of the horse, in its blind spot, it may move away and you will lose your hold on it.

g.   Lead it in keeping by its shoulder, encouraging it to walk on beside you and not to lag behind. Don't restrict the horse's head but hold the rope close to the head collar to give maximum control if needed. Never wrap a rope around your hand. If the horse pulls, the rope will tighten and you are likely to be trapped and injured.

Leading in hand

h.   Most gates open into the field to help to prevent horses from barging out. You can teach your horse to step back as you open the gate.

i.   Always give the horse plenty of room in the gateway. If the gate hits its side, it will soon start to rush through gateways out of fear of being hurt.

j.   Close the gate securely behind you.

2. Tying Up

a.   It is advisable to tie horses to a piece of string, rather than directly to a metal ring. The string should not break too easily but if the horse pulls hard in panic, it should give way. Once the horse has broken free it will probably soon relax. (It is important to have an enclosed yard, to prevent a loose horse from escaping.) If the horse cannot break free of the rope, it will go on panicking and may even throw itself to the ground, which could result in damaged limbs and wounds.

Tie up using a slip knot

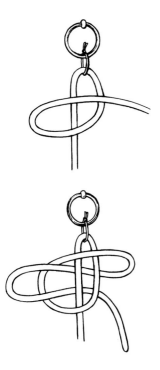

b. Tie up using a slip knot. You should always be able to release a horse quickly. Allow the horse enough rope to have free movement of its head, but not so much that it may get a leg caught over the rope. You may wish to tie the horse on a very short rope while grooming, especially if it is inclined to nip.

3. Handling

a. When approaching a tied-up horse, go quietly towards its shoulder, using the horse's name. As you move around the horse, to groom, tack up, etc., keep in contact with it by running a hand over its coat. In this way it will remain constantly aware of your presence. Unexpected movements will trigger the flight or fight instincts of the horse. If startled, it may, for example, pull back or kick out.

b. When grooming down the legs or putting on boots, never kneel down. Just squat down, so that you can move away quickly. Pick up a hind leg by running your hand down the front of the limb. Do not wrap your arm around the back of the limb, as you may get caught up if the horse kicks out.

c. The horse should be taught to move over on command. Place your hand on its flank or hindquarters and apply firm pressure, at the same time saying "Over". Repeat until you get the desired reaction. Praise the horse each time and it will soon move over willingly as soon as you give the command.

d. As it can be difficult to apply boots and bandages while the horse is resting a leg, it is also necessary to teach the horse to stand with its weight on all four feet when required. Using the "Over" command will often achieve this aim. Alternatively, you may need to ask the horse to step back. Stand in front and a little to one side of it. Place one hand on the head collar and one hand in the middle of the horse's chest with your thumb at the base of its neck and the rest of your hand pushing against it, at the same time saying "Back". Repeat the command until you get the desired result. Praise the horse and it will soon learn to respond to the command "Back".

e. Take note of how your horse reacts to you as you handle it. For example, it may threaten to bite you when you use a dandy

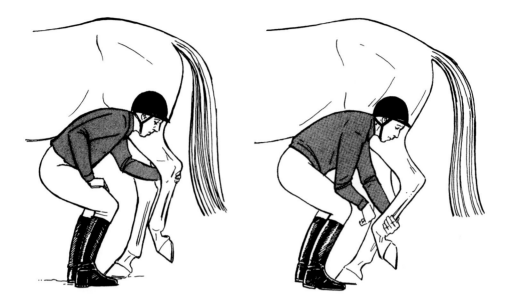

The correct technique for picking up a hind foot, avoiding wrapping your arm around the hind leg

brush on certain parts of its body. Don't just tell it off, as constant repetition of this problem is likely to make it resentful so that it bites and kicks more aggressively. Instead, you should look for a solution to the problem. Perhaps use a different brush or use the brush more gently or even more firmly, so that you do not irritate or tickle the horse in the first place.

4. Approaching a Horse

a. Always encourage the stabled horse to come to the door before you go into the stable. In this way you can go in, slip on the head collar and be in control of the situation.

b. If the horse will not come to the door, and especially if it turns its quarters towards you, encourage it with a handful of feed until it has learnt the habit of greeting you at the door. It should, however, step back immediately if you give the command "Back", to avoid the possibility of it barging out as you open the door.

c. Once in the stable with the head collar on, you can tie the horse up and adjust rugs, groom, muck out, etc. Remember to approach the tied-up horse as described above. Whatever part of the horse you need to approach, for example, a hind leg to put on a boot, always go to the shoulder first, then run your hand over the horse's coat to that area. Never just "dive in", as the horse may not be aware of your intentions.

- It is not advisable to take a bucket into the field, as it will immediately attract the atten-tion of all the horses

5. Leading and "Standing Up"

a. When leading a horse out of its stable for veterinary or other inspection, in order to have full control, especially as a vet may cause it to become agitated, it should be led out in a bridle. The handler should wear gloves and a hard hat and carry a stick if necessary.

b. Take care to lead the horse straight through the centre of the doorway. Do not try to turn the horse until it is completely clear of the doorway, as the horse's hips are particularly vulnerable if knocked against the side. If the horse is hurt in this way, it will begin rushing through doorways, which will exacerbate the likelihood of injury.

c. For inspection by the vet, potential purchaser, etc., the horse should be asked to stand with its weight supported squarely on all four feet. To achieve this, lead the horse in an active walk on a straight line. Steady the horse, then give the command "And stand". If it hasn't halted squarely, you can encourage each leg into position by

- Tie up using a slip knot. You should always be able to release the horse quickly asking the horse to step back or take another step forward, as necessary.

d. Stand in front of the horse, facing it and a little to one side. Take one rein in each hand to give you control. By not standing directly in front, you avoid being kicked by the horse if it strikes out with a forelimb.

e. As the person looking at the horse moves around it, from one side to the other, the handler should also move in order to be on the same side of the horse as that person. This also applies to a horse in the stable or tied up on the yard, etc. The idea is to minimise the risk of one person being kicked, stepped on or crushed by the horse swinging sideways or lashing out. For example, two people on the same side of the horse can move its quarters away from them by turning its head towards them.

f. Walk by the horse's nearside shoulder and look straight ahead. Do not move ahead of the horse nor turn to look at it. This will discourage the horse, making it more likely to resist.

- When approaching a tied-up horse, go quietly towards its shoulder, using the horse's name. As you move around the horse, keep in contact with it by running a hand over its coat

g. Use your voice to say "Walk on" or "Trot", and encourage the horse, if necessary, by using the stick in your left hand. Reach behind you and flick the horse's side or quarters.

h. One hand should hold the reins close to the bit, without restricting the horse's head. The other hand should hold the end of the reins so that they do not trail on the ground or get caught round your feet!

i. The horse is generally led from the nearside but it is useful for it to learn to be led from both sides.

j. By walking the horse positively on a straight line and not interfering with its head movement, observers will be able to see how the horse moves.

Ready to trot the horse up for inspection by the vet or other person. To aid control, the horse wears a bridle. The handler wears protective clothing: gloves, hard hat and boots

This photograph was taken under examination conditions at The Talland School of Equitation

k. When you turn the horse, turn it away from you. In this way you will maintain better control and balance. If you swing the horse around you, it can easily pull back and get away from you or step on you.

l. The same procedure applies to leading the horse in trot. Make sure, however, that the horse has returned to walk before you start to turn it and that it is completely straight after the turn before you ask it to trot again. Horses have been made to slip and

Leading the horse in hand for walking exercise. The horse wears a bridle to aid control, and boots for protection

This photograph was taken under examination conditions at The Talland School of Equitation

fall by handlers rushing into trot after a turn or not taking time to steady the horse before turning.

m. When you return the horse to the stable, turn it around to face the doorway and check that the door is closed before you remove the head collar or bridle. In this way you can slip out of the stable and will not risk being trapped in the corner of the box by a horse which has turned its hind legs towards you.

6. Turning Out

a. Wearing gloves and possibly a hard hat, lead your horse out to the field in a head collar and rope.

b. Keep hold of the gate as you lead the horse in, to minimise the risk of other horses escaping. Close the gate securely behind you.

c. Turn the horse to face the gate before you let it go. This will give you time to move away from the horse before it turns and moves off. Some horses rush off and kick out at the same time, so if you haven't had time to move away you could get kicked. You could offer the horse a titbit to discourage it from rushing off.

d. If several horses are being turned out, let them all go at the same time. This prevents a horse trying to pull away in its desire to follow another one that has been let loose.

e. Having let the horses go, don't chase them into the field. This will only encourage the horses to pull away and kick out.

f. Finally, no matter how well you know your horse, it is never worth taking risks with your safety. Horses are unpredictable and those with the quietest natures can sometimes behave badly. By handling all horses correctly and making sure that they respond in the right way, you will establish a good relationship with each horse. This should produce well-behaved horses and minimise the likelihood of accidents.

Follow-up Work to Confirm Knowledge and Experience

1. Working with a variety of horses, both stable- and grass-kept, on a daily basis is the best way to gain experience of horse behaviour.
2. Be strict with yourself about following safe and correct procedures and they will soon become second nature to you.
3. Whenever possible, observe other people handling horses. Ask yourself if their approach is safe and effective. If it is, follow their example; if not, learn from their mistakes.

Helpful Hints and Exam Technique

 Carry a hoof pick in your pocket at an exam, and make sure you always pick out a horse's feet before leading it out on to the yard. This demonstrates a practical and time-saving approach to keeping the yard tidy.

Make sure you take gloves, a whip and hard hat to the practical sections of the exam. Always put on gloves and hat to lead the horse, and ask for your whip if the horse is lazy when being led.

If a bridle is not provided for leading, ask if there is one available. Don't forget to use your voice to help the horse to understand you. A clear command of "Walk on" or "Trot" shows confidence and helps to establish a rapport with the horse.

Where appropriate, talk from your own experience. For example, when talking about catching, you may know a horse which will only be caught if you catch its friend first. This helps to demonstrate your practical experience.

3 Grooming

1. Reasons for Grooming

a. To clean the horse thoroughly, which will also stimulate the horse's circulation and promote health.
b. To improve the appearance of the horse.
c. To aid the prevention of disease.
d. To help build a relationship with the horse.

2. The Grooming Kit

a. Hoof pick – For removing packed-in dirt and stones from the hoof. Used from the heel towards the toe to prevent the point of the hoof pick accidentally digging into the frog or heels.
b. Dandy brush – For removing dry mud from the coat. Usually used on unclipped, less sensitive parts of the body and on the legs if care is taken not to knock the bony parts of the limbs. The dandy brush should not be used on the mane and tail as it will break the hairs. Use in short, firm strokes.
c. Body brush – For removing grease and dust from the coat. Generally used on stable-kept horses, all over the body, including the mane and tail. Used more sparingly on the grass-kept horse as it needs to keep the grease in its coat to protect it from the weather. Being soft, it is the best brush to use on the horse's face and any other sensitive areas. It is used in conjunction with the metal curry comb. When using the body brush on the nearside of the horse, hold it in your left hand, and in your right hand when on the offside. This enables you to put more strength into the slightly semi-circular movement with which the brush should be firmly applied.
d. Metal curry comb – For removing grease from the body brush. It is never used on the horse. After each stroke, the body brush

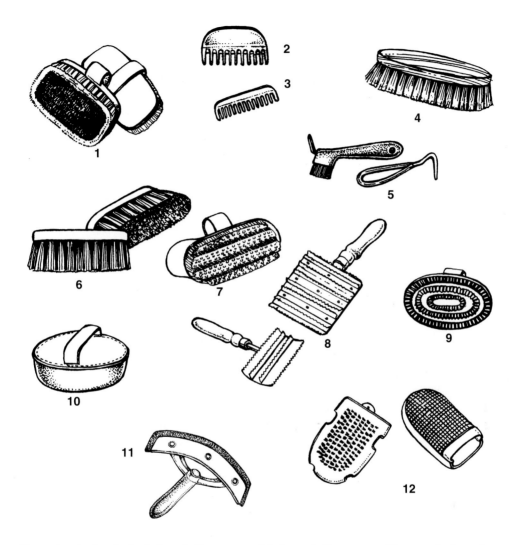

Grooming tools: **1**=*body brush;* **2**=*mane and tail comb;* **3**=*mane pulling comb;* **4**=*water brush;* **5**=*hoof picks;* **6**=*dandy brush;* **7**=*plastic curry comb;* **8**=*metal curry combs;* **9**=*rubber curry comb;* **10**=*leather wisp or massage pad;* **11**=*sweat scraper;* **12**=*grooming mitts*

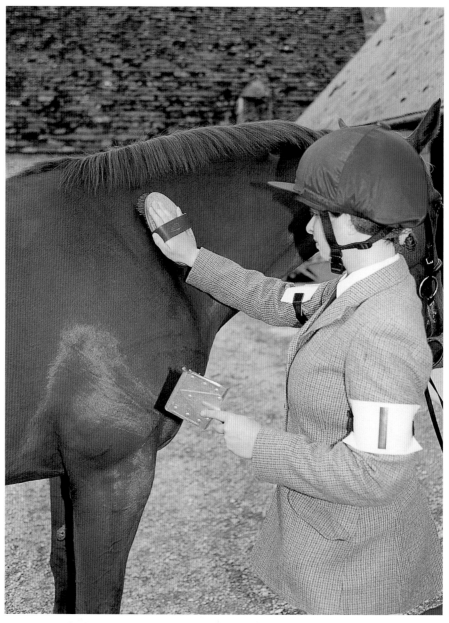

Grooming the horse with body brush and curry comb

This photograph was taken under examination conditions at The Talland School of Equitation

should be drawn across the curry comb which is held in the opposite hand. The grease is then knocked from the curry comb by tapping it on the ground.

e. Rubber curry comb – For removing grease from the coat. Normally used on stable-kept horses, all over the body. Firmly applied in small circles, against the lie of the hair, it brings the grease to the surface.

f. Plastic curry comb – For removing mud and the loose winter coat during moulting. It is generally used on grass-kept horses, all over the body. It should not be used on the mane and tail as it will break the hairs. It can be used in any kind of stroke necessary to remove the mud and loose coat. Also used to clean the body brush, it makes a good and safe substitute for the metal curry comb, especially for children.

g. Mane comb – For removing tangles from the mane. It may also be used on the tail. It is used in a simple combing action, taking a small portion of hair at a time. The smaller combs with short teeth are for mane pulling.

h. Stable rubber – For removing dust from the surface of the horse's coat after grooming. It can be used all over the horse, just like a duster.

i. Grooming mitt – For removing grease and dust from the horse's coat. It can be used on any part of the horse's body, including the head. A mitt is generally made of cactus cloth or rubber. Both types are stroked firmly over the body or used in a circular or to and fro action to remove dried sweat, mud, etc. The rubber type will lift grease to the surface, while the cactus cloth type will lift off surface grease/dust and help to create a shine on the coat.

j. Cactus cloth – Has the same use as the grooming mitt described above, but is in the form of a duster-sized cloth.

k. Water brush – For applying water to the coat/mane/tail in order to lay the hair or to wash it. It can be used on any part of the horse, including the feet.

l. Sponges – For washing the horse's eyes, nostrils and under the dock. You should have two separate sponges, one for each area, in different colours to avoid confusion.

m. Sweat scraper – Used to remove excess water from the horse's coat. When the horse has been bathed or washed down the

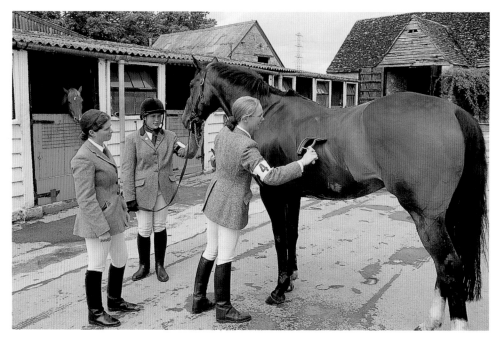

Using the sweat scraper

This photograph was taken under examination conditions at The Talland School of Equitation

rubber edge of the sweat scraper is used on the more bony parts of the horse, like the legs, and the harder metal or plastic edge is used over the main, smooth, muscle areas of the body. The scraper is drawn across the body following the lie of the hair and excess water is scraped off.

3. Some General Points

a. Always tie your horse up before grooming. You do risk being cornered in the stable and may be kicked or bitten, especially if you are grooming a sensitive spot.

b. Remove water buckets before you begin grooming. Dust created during the grooming process will quickly make the water dirty. If the stable has an automatic water drinker, clean out the bowl when you have finished grooming.

c. All brushes can be used in a to and fro action, against the lie of the hair, to help to remove mud, grease, etc. However, you should always finish with a stroke that lays the hair flat in its direction of growth.

d. Brushes will not remove grease and mud from a wet coat, so leave a wet horse to dry before grooming.

e. When grooming the head, first untie the horse. Stand facing the horse. With one hand holding the head collar, use the other hand to body brush the front of the face. Start in the middle of the forehead and work upwards and outwards, and then down to the end of the nose. Then slip the head collar back around the horse's neck. To groom the nearside of the face, stand with your right shoulder under the horse's throat, put your right arm around the offside of its face and place your hand on its nose. Your left hand is then free to brush the face. Repeat on the other side. Then replace the head collar and tie up.

f. The head collar should never be put around the horse's neck while the rope is tied to the wall. If the horse steps back or is startled, the head collar may tighten around its throat or slip over its head, causing the horse to panic and maybe break loose. Untie the rope first and either place it over the horse's neck or leave it loose in the string loop.

g. To groom the mane, brush all of it over on to the opposite side to that on which it normally lies. With the body brush or mane comb, bring a few hairs at a time towards you and brush thoroughly to remove dirt and tangles. Start at the poll and work towards the withers until you have groomed the whole mane.

h. To groom the tail, stand to one side of the horse, never directly behind it. Stand close in to the horse's quarters and take the whole tail in one hand. With the other hand, use the body brush to brush down a few hairs at a time. Difficult tangles can be loosened with your fingers. You can work through the whole tail with your fingers if you prefer.

• Always tie the horse up for grooming, to prevent accidents like being kicked or bitten, and remove from the grooming area water buckets to avoid them being dirtied with dust and hair.

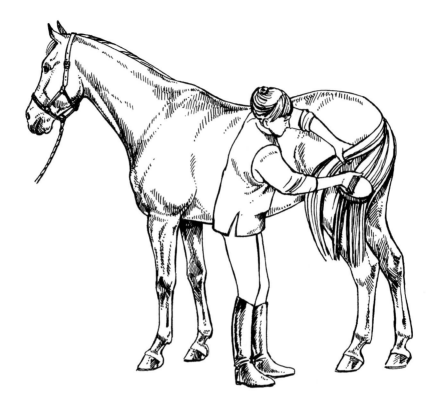

Grooming the tail

   i.   If your horse is quite tall, stand on a stool or box to make sure you get all of it really clean.

   j.   While grooming, constantly run your spare hand over the horse. In this way you will feel dirt, scabs, lumps, heat, etc., that may be forming, for example under the hair or under the belly and which are not visible. This is especially important when grooming the legs. You should constantly compare the two forelegs and the two hind legs, as this will help you to detect abnormalities at the earliest possible stage.

   k. Use your grooming time to learn about every inch of your horse.

   l.   Always put loose hair, and pick out feet, into a skip to keep the yard area tidy.

m. Wash the whole grooming kit regularly. If you are using it every day, it will probably need to be washed once a week. Wash it in warm, soapy water. Washing-up liquid will do the job. Be careful not to leave wooden or leather-backed brushes soaking as these materials will soon rot or crack. Wash and rinse the brushes clean of soap then leave them to drain and dry in a warm atmosphere.

4. Method

Grooming is the basic cleaning of the horse. It is the term generally used when referring to the preparation of the grass-kept horse/pony or stabled horse/pony for work.

a. Pick out feet. It is always best to do this dirty job first so you don't end up spreading dirt onto areas already groomed, and so you can check the horse's shoes are all present and in suitable condition for riding.

b. Remove mud and loose coat with the dandy brush and plastic curry comb. If the horse has a fine summer coat and sensitive skin, these brushes may be too harsh and you will need to miss this stage and move onto the next.

c. Groom the mane and forelock with the body brush and/or mane comb. Your fingers can also be a useful tool for removing tangles. Always use a soft brush on the mane to prevent hairs being broken, which causes the mane to become thin and straggly. Groom the mane and forelock before grooming the face and body of the horse, as dirt will fall out of the mane onto the coat.

d. Groom the head with the body brush.

e. Groom all over the body and legs with brushes appropriate for that particular horse. This usually entails working over the horse with the rubber curry comb to lift grease from the coat, followed by using the body brush with metal curry comb to remove all the grease. Remember not to remove too much grease from the coat of a grass-kept horse/pony. It may

• Use your grooming time to learn about every inch of your horse, feeling for lumps and bumps and sensitive areas which may be a sign of injury or disease.

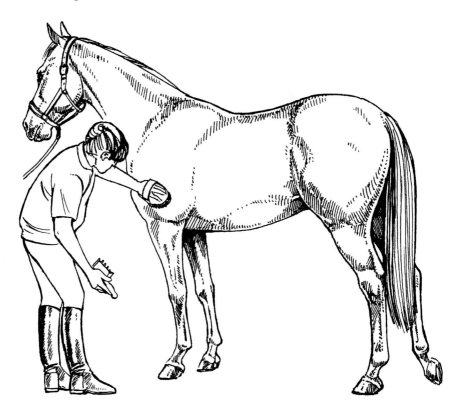

Groom all over the body and legs of the horse

only be necessary to work over the whole body with a dandy brush in this case.

f. Groom the tail with body brush and your fingers.

g. Finally, wash the eyes, nostrils and under the dock.

Follow-up Work to Confirm Knowledge and Experience

1. Working in a yard where there are both stable- and grass-kept horses that need grooming every day is the best way to become practised and efficient at the job.

2. Many new designs and items of grooming kit are constantly

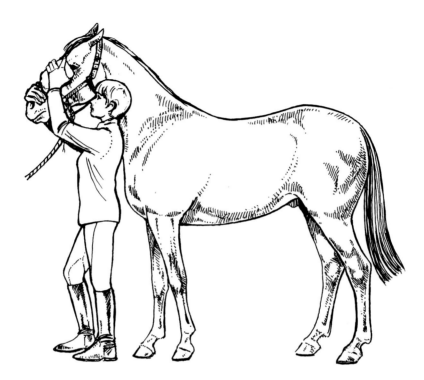

Sponging the eyes and nostrils

coming on to the market. Visit a local saddlery shop where you can look at, and familiarise yourself with, any new designs.

Helpful Hints and Exam Technique

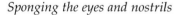 Remember that your hands are your best grooming tool. Make sure you do not wear gloves when grooming because you need to be able to feel for lumps, bumps, heat, etc.

Always groom with vigour, even if you are just briefly demonstrating the use of a certain brush.

If you need to go in and out of the stable for equipment, always close and bolt the door behind you even if the horse is tied up.

 It is easy to forget safe procedures when handling a quiet horse, especially if you know the horse quite well. In the exam, treat each horse as if you have never met it before. Don't walk or stand directly behind the horse. Don't make sudden or careless movements. Keep safety uppermost in your thoughts. Remember to replace the water buckets when you have finished and before you untie the horse.

4 Bedding and the Mucking Out Procedure

1. Bedding Systems

a. Complete mucking out – All the soiled bedding is removed every day and the floor swept clean, therefore all the bedding is moved. It would take an experienced person 15–20 minutes to muck out an average-sized stable.

b. Deep litter – With minimum disturbance of the bedding, all the droppings and very wet patches are removed. The remaining bedding is levelled out and clean bedding is placed on top. This is a less time-consuming process than complete mucking out, taking only 10–15 minutes. A deep base provides warmth and protection. However, it would not be practical to allow the base to become deeper than approximately 20–25 cm (8–10 in), so the entire bed will need to be removed every three or four weeks. This is hard, time-consuming work if done manually. Stables designed with tractor access make the process easier.

c. Combined system – It may suit your lifestyle to deep litter your stable during the week and muck it out completely at the weekend.

2. Types of Bedding

a. Straw – Probably the most commonly used bedding, straw is relatively inexpensive and fairly easy to dispose of. There are three types of straw:

- Wheat – which is best, being the most resilient.
- Barley – which is a little less tough.
- Oat – which is not as suitable as it is soft and very palatable.

A good sample of straw should be clean, free from mould and strong-stemmed, thus allowing moisture to drain through the bed and leaving the horse with dry standing on top.

b. Shavings – A popular bedding for horses that are inclined to eat straw and also for those that have respiratory allergies. It is more expensive than straw and difficult to dispose of if you are using large amounts. A shavings bed is more absorbent than a straw one and must be well handled to prevent it from becoming soggy. A good bale should contain large clean shavings, a minimum of dust and no debris, such as pieces of wood, etc. If purchased in plastic-wrapped bales, shavings can be stored outside. This is a great advantage if barn space is limited.

c. Paper – A dust-free, inedible bedding, particularly suited to horses with respiratory problems. It comes in the form of diced or shredded newspaper. However, most people find it difficult to work with. Being very absorbent, it can become packed down and difficult to remove unless the bed is frequently "fluffed-up", as it does not have the "spring back" quality of straw and shavings. If purchased in plastic-wrapped bales, it can also be stored outside.

d. Rubber – Now popular in horse boxes and trailers, where it has taken over from conventional bedding, but not yet a very popular form of flooring for stables. It is considered more hygienic, more slip-resistant, warmer and harder wearing than conventional flooring. In the stable it can be labour saving and eliminates the daily/weekly/monthly problem of bedding disposal. Many owners feel that rubber on its own doesn't provide necessary warmth and comfort, while others argue that horses lie down happily in the field and don't need the comfort of soft bedding. In trials, some horses appear to feel the cold more, some lie down as often as before, and others less so. Used without bedding, the rubber flooring can be washed down each day. Droppings need to removed frequently to prevent the horse from

- When mucking out, throw away as little bedding as possible. Leave the bed clean but be aware that bedding is expensive and the cost of its replacement considerable.

A horse stabled on a paper bed in a large stable

getting very dirty when lying down. Rubber can be used with conventional bedding but, being a softer than normal flooring, it only requires a thin layer of straw, shavings, etc.

3. Some General Points on Mucking Out

a. The door of the stable must always be securely hooked back during mucking out. If left swinging, it could hit a passing horse or person, frighten a horse or be broken. Always secure doors.

Long or short
handled four-
pronged fork

yard brooms

shovel

wheelbarrow

shavings fork

skip and rake for droppings

Mucking out tools

b. The positioning of the wheelbarrow requires some thought. If the horse is not in the stable there is no problem and the wheelbarrow can be brought into the stable to save making a mess on the yard. If the horse is in the stable, you must take care that the wheelbarrow is not protruding into the stable where the horse may swing round and catch itself on the handles, for example. So, depending on the size of the stable and where the horse is tied, either place the wheelbarrow across the doorway, sideways on, or just inside the doorway with the handles away from the horse.

c. Throw away as little bedding as possible. It is expensive and cost should always be considered. Disposal of bedding can be difficult, so don't add to the problem unnecessarily.

d. Choose a different wall to pile the clean straw against each day. In this way no part of the floor goes unswept for longer than a day or two at a time.

e. Keep yard sweeping to a minimum by loading your wheelbarrow correctly. As you muck out, fill the four corners of your wheelbarrow first. This creates a dip in the middle into which the last shovelful of droppings can be placed. In this way, you will not leave a trail behind you as you take your wheelbarrow to the muck heap.

f. If the horse is in the stable while you muck out, safety should be your first thought. The stable tools have the potential to injure the horse and the horse could then injure you. The horse must be tied up. However well behaved it is, it may be startled by external influences. This could lead to it barging into you and the tools or perhaps trying to jump out over the wheelbarrow – a potentially disastrous situation!

g. While working around the horse, make sure you keep the tools, especially the fork, well away from it. Move the horse over to stand on the opposite side of the box to the one at which you are working.

h. If the horse is going out of its stable to work or to be turned out, the bed could be left up to allow the floor to dry or be disinfected.

i. If the horse is staying in its stable, the bed should be put down. Lay the remaining bedding evenly over the floor, then top up with approximately half a bale of fresh straw/shavings. Build banks around the edges to prevent injuries or the horse getting cast and to minimise draughts. The bed should be thick enough to protect the horse from the concrete floor. If the flooring is easily exposed when the horse moves around, the bed is too thin. Overly thick beds are wasteful and time consuming.

j. Some owners prefer to use a "day bed" and "night bed". After mucking out some of the bedding is laid, to make a slightly thinner bed that can be easily skipped out during the day. In the evening the rest of the bed is laid and fresh bedding is added, to make a thick night bed.

k. If the bed is skipped out frequently throughout the day, and again at evening stables, the job of mucking out the next morning is much easier.

4. Full Mucking Out Procedure for a Straw Bed

a. Assemble the tools: four-prong fork, broom, shovel and wheelbarrow.

b. Remove the horse from the stable or tie up securely in the stable.

Use the fork to remove piles of droppings

c. Hook back the door and place the wheelbarrow across or just inside the doorway, with the handles pointing away from the horse.

d. Remove the obvious piles of droppings with the fork. To do this, lift the straw under the droppings with the droppings on top, then tip the droppings into the wheelbarrow and replace the clean straw in the bed. Alternatively, put on rubber gloves and remove the droppings by hand.

e. Next choose one wall against which to put all the clean bedding. Work around the stable, tossing all the clean straw into a pile against this wall and placing all the soiled straw and droppings in the wheelbarrow.

• If the horse's bed is skipped out frequently throughout the day, and again at evening stables, the job of mucking out the next morning is much easier

f. Use the broom to sweep the floor clean and then shovel up the remaining debris.

g. Now put the straw back down as a bed.

h. Top up with fresh bedding.

i. Empty the wheelbarrow and put away the tools.

j. Untie the horse and check that it is securely bolted into its stable

5. Variations for Full Mucking Out of a Shavings Bed

a. Wearing rubber gloves, remove the obvious droppings by hand, placing them straight into a skip. If you prefer, this can be done with a shavings fork.

b. Work through the whole bed with a shavings fork, removing the soiled patches and putting the clean bedding to one side.

6. Building and Maintaining a Muck Heap

a. If the muck heap is well packed down, it will rot more quickly. As it rots it will reduce in size. This helps to keep the muck heap at a manageable size.

When making a muck heap it is not just a case of anyhow and anywhere will do. The muck heap (above) has been "squared up" and (below) students work to keep a muck heap in good order. This is the safe and tidy way of dealing with waste in stables

b. Rotting muck heaps become very hot and can self-ignite, therefore it is essential to position the muck heap at a safe distance from buildings, although, at the same time, it should be easily accessible for workers with wheelbarrows, tractors and lorries.

c. A tidy muck heap will aid rotting, reduce the risk of it becoming a fire hazard and improve the appearance of the yard.

d. Empty the wheelbarrow into the back of the muck heap area or toss the contents of the wheelbarrow on top of the existing muck heap.

e. Using a fork, level and beat down the top of the muck heap, straightening the front as you go. This process is termed "squaring off".

f. As the heap increases in size, it is helpful to climb on top and trample it down.

7. Muck Heap Disposal

a. The method of disposal depends upon the size of the muck heap, type of bedding, location and facilities.

b. In some areas, mushroom farmers will remove straw muck heaps for a small fee, providing there is a large enough quantity to make it worthwhile.

c. A well-rotted muck heap may be mixed with farmyard manure and spread on fields as fertiliser. It is not suitable for fertilising grazing intended for horses because of the likelihood of spreading worm larvae and increasing the worm burden on the field.

d. Small muck heaps can be kept burning, providing the prevailing winds keep the smoke away from the yard and your neighbours. However, this practice is not environmentally friendly.

e. Shavings muck heaps are more difficult to dispose of as they take much longer to rot down.

Follow-up Work to Confirm Knowledge and Experience

1. Working on a regular basis in a yard or yards where there are stabled horses on a variety of bedding is the best way to become efficient at handling the tools and mucking out.

2. Try using different methods, such as a deep litter, and different

Forking the contents of the wheelbarrow on to the muck heap

techniques, such as rubber gloves and skip, in order to gain first-hand experience of the systems that best suit you and your horses.

Helpful Hints and Exam Technique

In any practical part of the exam, make sure you skip out the horse's box as soon as there are any droppings. This demonstrates that you are aware of good working procedure and is the only practical course of action as no one should want to stand and work in piles of droppings.

❧ Remove water buckets before you demonstrate any part of the mucking out procedure, or check and clean an automatic water bowl when you have finished.

❧ If you prefer to use rubber gloves for skipping out, then take a pair with you in your coat pocket.

5   Horse Psychology

By learning about the natural instincts of the horse and how domesticated horses of different types and ages may behave in various situations, and also why they do so, we can begin to understand equine behaviour. This, in turn, will aid safe and effective working practices with the horse as well as helping the individual to cope with horses which have developed behavioural problems. It will also encourage us to create a happy environment for the horse, which will help to minimise the likelihood of horses developing behavioural problems in the first place.

1.   Natural Instincts and Lifestyle

a.   The basic instincts to survive and reproduce govern the behaviour of the horse. The strongest, most dominant stallion will gather a group of mares and endeavour to protect them. There will also be a dominant mare who will lead the group.

b.   Horses are sociable animals, living together as a herd. Led by the dominant mare and stallion, stronger or weaker herd members will establish their place, resulting in an order similar to the "pecking order" among chickens. Many smaller groups of friends will also form within the herd.

c.   Horses are not predatory animals, but would have been preyed upon in the wild. They instinctively flee from danger, using their speed to escape from their attacker. It is important that the whole herd should keep together if danger threatens as groups are less vulnerable to attack than individuals. Therefore, if one horse takes flight, the whole herd will respond and go too.

d.   The horse's sense of hearing is very acute. Their mobile ears constantly move to listen for danger that may approach from any direction. Likewise, their eyes are set on the sides of their faces for good peripheral vision. They have a small blind spot immediately behind and in front of them but can move their heads around in order to see if predators are approaching. The horse's

Horses relaxed and grazing in the field

head and ear movements are a constant indication of what it is thinking and feeling.

e. If cornered and unable to take flight, the horse will try to defend itself. It can turn its hind legs towards the attacker and lash out or can bite and strike out with a foreleg.

f. Horses graze throughout the day, keeping the stomach supplied with food but never letting it become full. This enables them to take flight at any time without having the restriction of a full stomach pressing against their lungs.

g. Horses rest by sleeping on their feet. Again, they can quickly take flight from this position. However, if the weather is fine and the

All horses enjoy rolling

    sun shining, they like to lie down providing there is no imminent threat of danger. One or more members of the group will remain standing, as "lookouts" for the herd.

h. All horses enjoy rolling. It helps to remove old winter coat and camouflages the horse by covering it in mud.

i. A horse can scratch many parts of its body with its teeth. However, as it cannot reach its own withers, it will approach and scratch the withers of another horse. This will stimulate the other horse into reciprocal scratching.

j. Colts and fillies will be boisterous together. Through play, they learn about adult behaviour and mutual respect.

k. Older horses will tolerate playful youngsters unless they become particularly boisterous. They may then bite or kick to establish their superiority and put the youngster in its place.

2. The Domesticated Horse in the Field

In many ways field-kept horses have a fairly natural lifestyle.

a. They will take flight as a herd if danger threatens.

b. They will take turns lying down and keeping watch.

Mutual scratching has benefit for both participants

Young horses like to play

The horse may display aggressive behaviour as demonstrated in these two examples: (right) ears back, tail raised, and head thrust forward; (below) charging, with mouth open and ready to bite

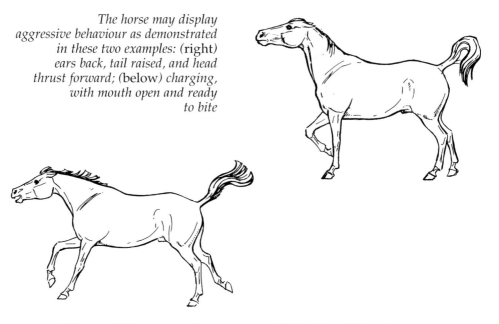

c. They will form smaller groups of friends within a large group.

d. They will establish who is the strongest and therefore the leader.

e. When relaxed, they will be seen grazing, spread out across the field, standing nose to tail swishing flies from each other's faces or scratching each other's withers.

f. If one horse is standing alone and obviously separate from the herd, not appearing to join in with the others, you should suspect something is wrong and investigate the situation. Likewise, if all the horses suddenly took flight across the field and began galloping around, you should look for the cause.

g. Mares and geldings should be separated in the spring and summer. This helps to prevent injuries occurring when geldings begin to behave like stallions by singling out mares in season and also fighting with each other.

h. After its companions have been taken away, a horse left on its own in the field may panic. It will call, trot up and down the fence and possibly try to jump out as instinct tells it to follow the herd. The same situation is likely to occur if two particular friends are separated, despite there being other companions available. However, horses soon adjust to being taken in and out of the field, providing more than one is left behind for company.

i.   One young and one old horse kept together may not enjoy each other's company. The young one will want to play, which may bother the older horse. However, several youngsters kept together will play happily, while older horses graze and rest quietly.

j.   In wet and windy weather, or when hot and bothered by flies, the horses will group together in sheltered areas. A horse alone in these conditions will either be wet and miserable with cold, without its companions to help to shelter it, or will run around the field in distress trying to escape flies that it cannot defeat on its own.

k.   In the confines of the field, a stronger horse may corner a weaker member of the group and defensive behaviour will be seen. The horses will kick out at each other or use their teeth to bite. Those with a more timid nature may try to jump out of the field rather than defend themselves.

l.   If a new horse is introduced to an established group, there will be a period of adjustment. This horse will have to establish its place in the herd. If it is quite dominant in nature, there may be a lot of fighting if it challenges the leaders of the herd. If it is more timid in nature, it will probably settle quite quickly, not posing a threat to any of the others. Initially, the rest of the herd will gather together and approach the new arrival. They will smell each other and there is likely to be kicking, squealing and some cantering around. The new arrival will also spend some time exploring its new surroundings. It will take at least a day to settle in.

m. If a horse has, for some reason, been stabled for a long period, it will take great delight in being returned to the more natural environment of the field. Typical behaviour includes galloping, rolling, exploring the field, smelling droppings left by other horses, bucking, snorting and, with all the senses alert, surveying its new surroundings.

3. Horses that are Difficult to Catch

Some horses become difficult to catch as soon as the spring grass comes through. Others develop a mistrust of people and learn that they can avoid being caught and thereby escape ill-treatment. Some stabled horses, which are only turned out occasionally, can be difficult to catch when they are given their freedom. There are many different ways of catching these horses. The method employed depends on the horse and the situation.

a. The horse's attitude, particularly its ears, will give you an indication of how easy or difficult it may be to catch. Ears back and swinging its head towards you in a threatening attitude is an obvious indication of its unwillingness. The same attitude is seen when one horse warns another not to come near feed, for example.

b. The horse may simply walk away or, if being more threatening, turn its quarters towards you, ready to kick.

c. The natural instinct to follow the herd can be helpful. If all the other horses in the field can be caught and brought into the yard, the last horse often allows itself to be caught in order to go with the herd.

d. In the same way, a loose horse may follow its friends in from the field and allow you to catch it when it reaches the stables. This only works if the track from field to yard is secure and not open to the road, for example.

e. A bucket of feed can be a good tempter, providing there are no other horses in the field.

f. If you leave a head collar on in the field, make sure it is a leather one which will break if the horse gets caught up. Attach a short piece of string, approximately 30 cm (1 ft) long, to help you to take hold of the horse when you go to catch it.

g. Some horses will give in if you are persistent and follow them around for long enough.

h. For horses which are particularly difficult, a very small turn out paddock can be a good compromise.

i. Try to prevent this annoying vice by making sure that your horse enjoys itself when caught, for example give a feed and don't always work the horse. Also make sure that stabled horses are turned out frequently.

4. The Stabled Horse

Being confined in a stable is the most unnatural way of life for a horse. As a result, problems and vices often develop.

a. If stabled, the horse should be provided with an environment in which it feels safe and where it can be provided with its daily needs.
b. A horse that is happy in its stable will appear relaxed, eat well, greet its owner at the door, lie down, or doze while standing, and generally display normal behaviour.
c. Confined to a stable, the horse cannot take flight if threatened. Its only option is to defend itself by biting or kicking. To prevent this dangerous behaviour, it is very important that we handle the horse in a quiet, kind and confident manner, making it feel safe and relaxed in its stable.

The horse kicking out, another display of aggressive behaviour, will arise where it feels threatened or is frustrated by restrictions on its freedom of action

d. Signs of unhappiness or distress will include threatening the owner with ears back and teeth showing; swinging hindquarters towards the door; not eating; box walking and weaving; rushing to and fro in the box, pushing at the door and calling; passing loose droppings; jumping back and snorting at any movements or noise.

• A sound understanding of equine behaviour will enable candidates to work safely and effectively with horses. Understanding why the horse behaves as it does is the best way to learn how to react and respond in any situation.

e. Being separated from the herd can lead to stable vices like weaving and box walking, but careful planning can help to make the horse feel more relaxed. For example, American barn stabling allows the horses to see and smell each other so that they continue to feel like part of a herd.

f. Very young horses will not take kindly to being kept in individual boxes where their freedom and social activity are restricted. Keeping them together in barns can solve many problems. This system can help to preserve your grazing during wet, winter weather, while providing the youngsters with dry, sheltered conditions.

g. When we restrict its intake of feed, the horse's need to be almost constantly grazing may lead to vices like crib biting and wind sucking. By feeding little and often, with as constant a supply of hay/carrots/swede as possible for the horse to nibble, we can minimise these problems.

h. The horse's acute hearing will pick up anything happening around the yard. However, when confined to the stable it may not be able to see what is causing the noise. This may lead to the horse fretting and becoming nervous. For this reason, keep noise and disturbance to a minimum.

i. Consider the horse's temperament when deciding where to stable it. A stallion will want to see all activity as horses leave and enter the yard so that he feels he is watching over his herd.

A timid horse may be miserable stabled between two very dominant horses. Horses lacking confidence will fret if stabled where they can constantly see other horses leaving the yard, as this will make them feel that the herd is leaving without them.

j. Horses of a nervous disposition will benefit from being stabled where they can see several other horses and communicate with them. This should also help you to gain their confidence as they will be able to see that the other horses trust you.

k. When approaching a nervous horse in its box, encourage it to come to the door to greet you first. Perhaps offer a handful of grass (or carrot, etc.), to bring the horse to the door. Allow the horse to smell and identify you, then slip in and put on a head collar.

l. Don't attempt to go in and handle the horse without putting on a head collar. This could lead to the horse cornering you and you resorting to aggressive behaviour in order to escape. This will not be conducive to gaining the horse's confidence.

m. The aim is to handle the horse calmly and gently. Make your movements slow and gain the horse's confidence through handling it frequently, giving it time to get to know you and your yard routine.

n. "Routine" includes how you carry out tasks, not just the time at which you do them. This is particularly important when trying to gain the confidence of a nervous horse, or when teaching good behaviour to a young horse. For example, if you tie the horse up outside its stable to tack it up, keep to this routine. Don't suddenly change to tacking up inside the stable, or vice versa.

o. One of the most important points of good horsemastership is to treat each horse as an individual. Different characteristics and behavioural problems require different approaches.

5. The Horse when Ridden

Many different factors will affect the horse's behaviour when ridden, for example the mood and character of both horse and rider, as well as the situation and task to be tackled. Remember that, when handling horses, we take the place of the leader of the herd. If the horse is confident in us as its leader, it will do as we ask. When it loses confidence in us, problems begin.

Riding Out/Hacking

a. While all horses will spook at times, some horses seem to be far spookier than others. This may be due to a lack of confidence in their rider or they may just be a naturally timid horse.

b. If the rider is nervous, the horse will feel this and become nervous itself, its instinct telling it that if the rider is worried then there must be danger around the corner.

c. When being ridden through the countryside, your horse will be on a constant lookout for danger. Bushes, hedges and banks could all be places where a predator may be hiding, therefore it may be reluctant to approach or may try to give such things a wide berth. A confident rider will reassure the horse by riding forward calmly but firmly. Hitting or shouting at the horse will only worry it and make the problem worse.

d. A nervous horse is likely to become nappy, spooky, buck, jog, etc. Again, the horse's ears will be the rider's main indicator of what it might be thinking.

e. Many horses learn that, with some riders, when they spook they temporarily unbalance their riders and escape from being between leg and hand.

f. If the rider is not quick to regain command of the situation, the horse will take charge.

g. If the rider is confident and clear in their commands, the horse will settle and gradually gain confidence.

h. The herd instinct will lead to problems if you try to separate horses while out on a hack. Likewise, if one horse shies at an object, all the other horses will shy too.

i. A young horse will be in particular need of a confident rider as it will be experiencing many strange sights and sounds for the first time.

j. A nappy horse is one which tries to go against its rider's wishes by refusing to go in a particular direction, down a particular path or over a particular obstacle. As the argument goes on, it will also buck and/or rear as well as run backwards or try to rush off in a different direction.

k. Many ponies nap to a lesser degree by dragging their young rider back to their stable or back to the gate, despite the young rider's attempts to stop them.

l. Napping generally starts when the horse or pony realises that the rider is not in control. Some horses take charge and refuse to move or take the rider to the nearest feed bucket. In this situation, the horse is not frightened, just a dominant character with a weak rider.

m. If the horse realises that the rider is not in control and becomes frightened by the situation, then the nappy reaction is likely to be more extreme. If a confident rider takes over, the horse will continue to nap until the new rider has rebuilt the horse's confidence.

n. The longer the horse has been getting away with being nappy, the longer it will take to put the problem right. In fact, it may never be possible to eradicate the problem completely.

o. Another cause of nappiness is discomfort. If the horse's tack doesn't fit, it has a problem with its teeth, a girth gall is forming or there is any other problem that causes pain and therefore fear, the horse is likely to nap in its attempts to get away from the problem. It is therefore advisable to try to eliminate any such possible causes before taking firmer action with the horse.

p. In some situations, nappiness may be due to overfeeding. If the horse is having little exercise and large amounts of concentrate feed, it may be so full of energy that it doesn't know what to do with itself. Consequently, it begins behaving badly. The first indication for the rider is when they get on the horse. If the horse is feeling tense, it may lift its back and feel as if it is about to buck. A swishing tail will also indicate tension.

q. Excess energy is often a reason for bucking. A horse full of fun and energy may buck to help itself let off steam, not just physically but also mentally.

r. Likewise, jogging can be a result

- The horse's attitude, particularly its ears, will give you an indication of how easy it will be to handle

of mental tension. For example, a highly-strung Thoroughbred, which has been hunting, may begin jogging when taken out on a hack, due to anticipating what it will be asked to do.

s. Jogging can also result from discomfort. The horse's instinct to take flight from danger leads it into trying to get away from whatever is hurting it. Pulling and snatching at the reins often accompanies the problem of jogging as the rider tries to restrain the horse and the horse tries to escape.

t. An unbalanced and not very good rider will cause the horse discomfort and this can lead to jogging, bucking or napping.

u. In all of these situations, the rider must first look carefully for the cause of the problem. It may be necessary to enlist the help of a second opinion from someone who can look at the problem objectively. Remove the cause then rebuild the horse's confidence.

v. Relieve tension in the horse by being careful not to overfeed and, once again, take care with your stable management. For example, turn out regularly, stable in a calm atmosphere with companionship and follow a regular exercise routine.

Follow-up Work to Confirm Knowledge and Experience

1. Keeping the horse's natural instincts uppermost in your mind, observe horses in as many different situations as possible – in the stable yard, in the field, at shows, at stud farms, at sales – and keep asking yourself why those particular horses are behaving in that particular way.

2. When working with your own horses, if you come across any problems, try to analyse how you could improve the horse's environment with due regard for natural instincts and see if you can successfully solve the problem.

Helpful Hints and Exam Technique

When answering questions in a theoretical situation, try to picture horses with which you have had experience. Whenever possible, answer the questions by using real examples. In this way your answers are more likely to have an authentic ring to them, showing the examiner that you really are experienced and have a good understanding of the subject.

Try not to disagree with other candidates' answers. If someone makes a statement with which you disagree, state your own opinion but remember that they may have experienced different situations to you and it may be that you are both correct. There are many situations in which there is no one correct answer, where everyone's comments can be valid.

6 The Field-kept Horse and Grassland Management

The needs of a horse at grass are many and varied. Through good management and regular maintenance, we can provide a horse with a suitable environment and good grazing. The field should have secure and safe fencing, shelter (either man-made or natural), and a constant water supply.

1. Fencing

General Points

a. The type of fencing you choose depends upon financial constraints, type of horse and existing fencing, hedges, etc.
b. Three rails or strands of wire will discourage horses from reaching through the fence. This reduces the likelihood of broken fences and escape.
c. The bottom rail/wire should be approximately 45 cm (18 in) from the ground. This allows horses to graze immediately under the fence but is too low for them to roll underneath it. If it is any lower than this, horses may get a foot caught over the bottom rail/wire.
d. The top rail/wire should be approximately 135 cm (53 in) high.
e. Posts are placed 5–6 m (16–19 ft) apart.
f. For Shetland ponies, you will need to lower these measurements, or use a different type of fencing, as Shetlands would escape easily under the bottom wire.
g. As horses are inclined to lean against fencing, wire and rails

Some of the problems caused by using unsuitable fencing

should be fixed to the inside of the posts, to prevent them from springing off.

Types of Fencing

a. Post and rail – Usually constructed of wood, although other materials, such as metal rails and concrete posts, can be used. Although expensive, post and rail provides a strong visible fence. The wood should be treated with a weatherproof preservative and will last longer if repainted each year. If the wood is not properly cared for and maintained it will rot, break and splinter, rendering it more easily broken by the inhabitants of the field, which could prove very hazardous.

b. Post and wire – Less expensive and therefore frequently used. Plain wire is best for horses, although it will stretch when leant

Good secure fencing. Rails should be fixed to the inside of the fence posts, to prevent them from springing off if horses push against them

on, therefore it should be frequently checked and made taut. Barbed wire may command more respect but poses a problem as it can cause horrific injuries. New Zealand rugs are frequently torn on barbed wire. Rail and wire are often combined with a top rail and two lower strands of wire, or a top and bottom rail with a strand of wire between.

c. Hedges – Providing the hedges themselves and any plants within them are not poisonous, they make good natural barriers which prevent horses from leaning against or reaching through the wire/rail with which they can be combined.

d. Electric – Initially, electric fencing was unsuitable for horses as it was a thin wire that they tended to run through and so become entangled. Now, reels of plastic fencing with thin strands of wire running through it are available. This fencing comes in broad strips and various colours, making it highly visible. It has insulators and joining buckles which make it possible to erect the fencing just like a post and rail. It has the advantage that horses will not lean on it.

e. Stud/stock fencing – This comes in various forms, the aim being to provide safe fencing for small, valuable foals, boisterous youngsters or any other horse for that matter. A wire mesh is used, with a close enough weave to prevent small feet from becoming trapped. This may be topped with a strip of rubber fencing which adds visibility and will not cause damage if run into.

f. Gates – As an essential part of the fencing, gates should open into the field, which helps to prevent horses from barging out, and should be wide enough for farm machinery to gain access. To deter thieves, the top hinge pin should be turned over to prevent the gate from being lifted off its hinges and the gate should be padlocked at both ends. Choose a latch that locks in place and cannot be opened by the horse.

2. Water

A constant fresh supply must be provided.

a. Natural sources – A running stream that comes from an unpolluted source is suitable, providing there is firm standing where the horses can approach. Any natural source that becomes stagnant, comes from a polluted area or has a very muddy approach should be fenced off and not used.

b. Self-filling trough – The most convenient way of supplying water to the field. The trough should be positioned away from trees, to prevent leaves and debris falling in, and away from the gate, to prevent crowding in this area, but close enough for easy checking. It should also be well away from the fence, to allow the horses to visit the trough without getting trapped, or form part of the fence in order to supply two fields at once.

c. Other systems – Various different troughs and buckets can be used and filled manually. The important points to remember are: the trough/bucket must be stable and not easily knocked over; there should be no sharp edges, handles or protrusions that a horse could be injured on; it must be cleaned and topped up frequently.

3. Shelter

Horses need protection from wind and rain in the winter and should be provided with shade in the summer.

a. Natural – Trees and hedges provide the best form of shelter for large groups of horses. They can then group themselves, without fighting, in the most sheltered or shaded part of the field.

b. Erected constructions – Suitable for smaller groups they should be positioned to protect horses from the prevailing wind. A three-sided construction allows for easy access, and also escape, through the open side. The shelter should be large enough to accommodate all the horses.

4. Maintaining Good Pasture

a. Areas of grass that taste sweetest to the horse are grazed very short, like lawns. If the field is overgrazed, these "lawns" become patchy and grazing is ruined for the future. Fields should be rested as the grass gets short, to allow for a period of regrowth. How often, and how long, the field is rested depends upon the number of horses grazing and the speed of regrowth. In spring, given warm weather and rain, the grass will grow rapidly.

b. Horses avoid grazing soured areas of grass where they have left their droppings. This creates a wasted area of long, rough grass. These "roughs" should be topped. This means that they are cut short in order to encourage dense growth, rather than sparse areas of long grass that the horses will continue to avoid grazing.

A three-sided field shelter allows for easy access

If available, sheep and cattle will top the long grass, being less fussy eaters than horses.

c. As well as making the grazing unpalatable to the horse, droppings contain worm larvae which will spread on to the grass, be eaten by the grazing horses and thus increase each horse's worm burden. If the paddock is small, the droppings should be removed daily. As this is not practical in large fields, they should be spread out with a harrow. Once spread, earthworms, rain, dung beetles, etc., will quickly work the droppings into the soil. At the same time, the larvae will be exposed to the weather and some may be destroyed before they can be eaten. A practical alternative to harrowing is available in the form of a large vacuum machine mounted on the back of a Land-Rover or tractor, which vacuums up the droppings.

> • The needs of a horse at grass are many and varied. Through good management and regular maintenance of pasture, the horse obtains most of its nutritional needs, worm damage is reduced to minimum levels, and the horse is provided with a safe environment.

d. Apart from removing the horses' droppings, the worm burden on the field can be reduced by periodically grazing sheep and cattle. They eat the horse worm larvae which are unable to survive in other animals, thus breaking the cycle and reducing the worm burden.

e. Plants like nettles and thistles will also need to be removed from the field. Although they are not poisonous, they will compete with the grass, leaving your field with more weed than grazing. Again, regular topping and/or grazing sheep and cattle will help to keep these plants, and others like them, under control. Many horses enjoy eating wilted thistles and nettles, so they can be left in the field when cut.

f. Seek advice about fertiliser from an expert, as this may be needed and should be applied in spring or autumn.

If you don't follow these procedures, you will end up with a horse-sick paddock. This is a paddock with obvious lawns and roughs, an excess amount of droppings, bare and poached areas and weeds and poisonous plants in abundance, and it will carry a very heavy worm burden.

5. Daily Checks

The grass-kept horse and its field must be checked several times every day. It only takes a few moments for a piece of fencing to be broken or for one horse to kick and injure another. Either of these incidents could have dire results if left unchecked for any length of time. Early-morning and late-evening checks are essential as the horse will have been, or will be about to be, left unseen through the night period. Throughout the day, look in on the horse as frequently as possible.

- Apart from removing droppings, the worm burden on the field can be reduced by periodically grazing sheep and cattle on the pasture.

    a. Check that the horse is behaving normally, shows no signs of ill health and has not sustained any injuries. Pick out its feet and check the shoes.

    b. If the horse is rugged, check that the fastenings are secure, replace the rug if it has slipped, look for tears and check that the rug is dry inside.

    c. Look at the fencing and gate. Are they secure?

    d. Is the water supply flowing and clean?

    e. Look for poisonous plants and weeds, especially in the spring.

    f. Make sure no debris has found its way into the field. There may be a tin can, plastic bag, etc. that needs removing.

    g. Shelters should be checked in case of broken boards or maybe a hole in the roof.

Follow-up Work to Confirm Knowledge and Experience

1. Try to put yourself in a situation where you can check field-kept horses on a daily basis so you become familiar with the sort of problems that may arise.

Helpful Hints and Exam Technique

When discussing field-kept horses, remember each candidate will have experience of different situations. Don't worry if they give different answers and have different ideas to you. Speak from your own experience.

7 Feeding

In order to become proficient at feeding suitable types and quantities of feed to a variety of different horses and ponies, it is necessary to recognise different feedstuffs, good and bad quality and understand the horse's nutritional needs.

1. The Rules of Feeding and Watering

a. Feed little and often – This method closely resembles horses' natural way of feeding. When not stabled, they graze and keep their relatively small stomachs constantly about half-full.

b. Only feed good quality feedstuffs – Poor quality feeds can contain mould spores which lead to respiratory disorders and are low in nutritional value, leading to unthriftiness in the horse.

c. Feed at regular intervals daily – Within the daily routine, horses soon learn to expect their feeds at certain times. Delay in feeding can lead to frustration and problems such as door banging. At competitions, normal feeding times may need to be adjusted. However, the change in routine, new surroundings, etc., should keep the horse occupied so it may not be so aware of the change in feeding times.

d. Use only clean receptacles to hold feed and water – Old food or debris of any sort left in the feed or water bowl will smell unpalatable and discourage the horse from eating the fresh food or drinking the water.

e. A supply of fresh water must be constantly available – Water is essential for all body functions. Approximately 70 per cent of the adult horse's bodyweight is water.

f. Do not feed directly before exercise – The stomach lies behind the diaphragm. When full, it will press against the diaphragm, restricting expansion of the lungs. At the same time, digestion will slow down as exercise starts. Allow a minimum of one hour after feeding before exercising.

g. Water before feeding – Although water should be constantly available, the horse will be deprived of it at times, for example during exercise. Therefore, on return, offer water before feed or the horse may be tempted to eat first, then drink a large quantity of water. This may cause the feed to swell rapidly, as well as diluting the digestive juices and washing feed rapidly through the system, leading to colic or poor digestion.

h. Change water buckets a minimum of three times daily – Water left standing in the stable will absorb ammonia. It should be tipped away and replaced with fresh water.

i. Do not make any sudden changes to the horse's diet – The horse has bacteria in its large intestine, which help to digest specific feeds. If new feeds are introduced gradually, the bacteria have time to adjust. Sudden changes will upset the bacterial balance, leading to poorly digested feed and colic.

j. Feed something succulent daily – Succulent feeds are enjoyed by the horse. When mixed with dry feeds, they improve mastication and digestion.

k. Feed plenty of bulk – As the horse's system is designed to digest large amounts, plenty of bulk and roughage are needed to aid digestion of all feeds and keep the system in good working order.

l. Give the horse water in small amounts on return from strenuous exercise – After an event or race, when the horse is hot and breathing heavily, water intake should be restricted. Offer it 2–3 litres (4–6 pt) at a time, every five minutes (take the chill off by adding some warm water to the bucket), until the horse has quenched its thirst. It can then be left with a normal water supply. This process prevents large amounts of cold water shocking the horse's system while it is returning to normal.

m. Feed according to the following factors:

- work being done
- age
- time of year
- whether grass-kept or stabled
- height and build
- ability of rider
- temperament

All these factors influence the type and quantity of feed. Harder work requires more energy-giving feed, while a laxative diet is needed if the horse is stabled and off work. Youngsters need body-building material; old horses may need softer, cooked foods that are easy to chew and digest. Grass-kept horses need food for warmth in winter, while those that are stabled can wear extra rugs. Larger horses need more feed than smaller ones but a large horse with a novice rider should not receive a high-energy diet which may make it difficult to manage. Whatever the size, age, etc., the temperament can vary. You should avoid giving oats to a more excitable type but may find that a more placid horse does very well on them.

2. Types of Feed

Hay – Some General Points

a. The quality of hay depends on when it was cut, how quickly it was dried, whether the pasture was free from weeds and the types of grass it is made from.

b. If the hay is cut early, the grass will still be very leafy and moist. A lengthy drying process may cause the leaf to disintegrate and make the hay very dusty. Large amounts of clover in the hay lead to the same problem. If cut too late, the grasses will have gone to seed and lost much of their nutritional value. At the same time, through exposure to wet weather, moulds may have started to form.

c. If dried quickly, the hay will maintain its nutritional value and contain little dust. However, if it rains and the hay is left out for several days, mould spores will multiply and the hay will quickly deteriorate and be very dusty.

d. Weeds reduce the feed quality of the hay and can be dangerous. Ragwort, for example, will be readily eaten when dried but is still poisonous. If it goes unnoticed in the hay ration, it could prove fatal.

e. Good quality grasses give the hay a higher nutritional value.

f. If hay is baled before it is sufficiently dry, it will heat up in the stack and moulds will form.

g. Visibly mouldy hay should not be fed to horses. The tiny mould spores will pass into the horse's lungs, causing inflammation and coughing.

h. The cleanest-looking hay can still carry mould spores. Soaking the hay in clean water will cause the mould spores to swell to a size that prevents them from being inhaled into the lungs, therefore it is advisable to feed soaked hay.

i. Good quality hay smells fresh, tastes sweet, looks clean and, when shaken out, doesn't appear to be dusty.

j. Poor quality hay will smell mouldy, look grey and dirty and be very dusty when shaken out. If you can see mouldy patches, it is very poor indeed.

k. Hay is a bulk feed. As the horse's digestive system is designed to digest large amounts of bulk, hay and its alternatives should form a large part of most horses' diets.

Meadow Hay

a. This is made from permanent pasture and contains a variety of grasses.

b. It is the type of hay most frequently fed to horses and is fairly soft and palatable.

Seed Hay

a. This is a crop grown from specially selected seeds. Rye grass is normally used.

b. Seed hay is quite a hard hay and more difficult to digest than meadow hay. However, providing it is well made, it has a higher nutritional value and is often used for competition horses.

Threshed Hay

a. This hay is grown from seed in order to produce more seeds that will be sold. It is cut and then threshed to remove the seeds.

b. Good quality grass will be used and, if well made, the hay can be

• The quality of the hay depends on when it was cut, how quickly it was dried, whether the pasture was free from weeds and the types of grass it is made from

of medium quality. The threshing process will have "battered" the grass and may make it more prone to being dusty.

Haylage

a. This is semi-wilted, vacuum-packed grass.
b. Once the air is excluded, a small amount of fermentation takes place but moulds do not form. This leaves a dust-free alternative to hay.

Oats

a. Oats have a thin outer husk that breaks away from the grain. This husk adds fibre to the diet and encourages the horse to chew the oats thoroughly.
b. A good sample should have an equal mix of husk and grain, rather than large amounts of husk. It should be free from dust and any sign of mould. The grain should be clean and fawn-coloured, with a white kernel.

Barley

a. A good sample of barley should be similar to oats but there will be no separate outer husk.

Maize

a. Whole maize is too hard and indigestible to feed. It is fed in a cooked, flaked form.
b. A good sample will consist of large firm flakes, yellow and white in colour. It should not be dusty, grey nor smell mouldy.

Sugar Beet

a. This product comes in dried and shredded or cubed form and must be soaked before it can be fed to horses. The shreds should be soaked overnight. Fill the container half full with shreds then fill almost to the top with cold water. The cubes should be soaked for longer, up to 24 hours, and require more water. Fill the selected receptacle one-third full of cubes and almost to the top with cold water.

b. A good sample will be sweet smelling, dark grey in colour and dry without being dusty.

Cubes

a. There are many different types of cube, each formulated as a balanced diet for horses and ponies in a particular type of work. For this reason, nutrient levels and energy values will vary.
b. A good sample should be dry so that each cube will break but not crumble.

Coarse Mixes

a. As with cubes, there are many different types, each formulated to provide the right balance of nutrients to horses and ponies in different types of work.
b. Good samples will be sweet and fresh smelling, with no traces of mould or dust.

Chaff

a. This is chopped hay or straw. You make the chaff yourself, although it can be bought in molassed form which is very popular as a tasty addition to feed.
b. It is added to concentrate rations to encourage the horse to chew the feed thoroughly. It will help to slow down the type of horse that bolts its feed, and also adds fibre to the diet.

Bran

a. This is a by-product, left over after the milling process of wheat. It should be dry and quite pink and white to look at, not grey or musty.

3. Deciding What to Feed

a. The examiner will expect you to be able to outline suitable types and quantities of feed for a stabled horse in light work and a field-kept horse or pony in light work.

Different feeds (starting at top left, reading clockwise): sugar beet cubes, horse and pony cubes, coarse mix, barley, oats, and soaked sugar beet

b. Light work is when a horse or pony is ridden at walk, trot and canter each day without being stressed.

c. Remember the horse or pony will need hay if stable-kept and hay in winter if grass-kept.

d. Horses are usually fed three times a day: morning, lunch and evening.

e. An average 16 h.h. horse will need approximately one section of hay at each feeding time. An average section of hay will weigh about 2 kg (4 lb). Therefore, it will receive 6 kg (12 lb) of hay per day.

f. If you put the hay in a hay net and weigh it, you will have an accurate record of how much you feed.

g. The grass-kept pony in winter will need a similar amount of hay, as some will be wasted when it is blown away or trampled into the mud. The pony at grass will also need plenty of food to help keep it warm, so it may even need more hay than the stabled horse, even though it is smaller.

h. As well as hay the stabled horse will need "hard" feed all year round. "Hard" or "concentrate" feed are terms used to describe the coarse mix, barley, cubes, etc., that are fed to the horse.

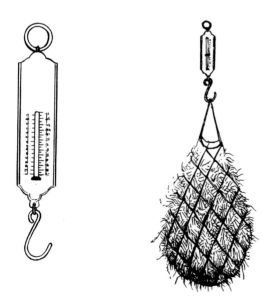

Use a spring balance to weigh out quantities to ensure accuracy when preparing feeds for different horses. Here hay is being weighed into a hay net

A good variety of feed is essential to ensure the good health and well-being of horses. Different feeds are illustrated in these two pages

Horse and pony nuts

Coarse mix

Rolled oats

Rolled barley

These two feeds are sugar beet, before and after soaking

Alfalfa

Bran

i.   Horses in light work usually do well when fed a low-energy coarse mix or cubes.

j.   Feed the horse three times a day, and use a scoop to measure the feed. A standard scoopful of coarse mix will weigh about 1.5 kg (3 lb). Check how much weight your scoop carries – remembering that different types of feed vary in weight. An average 16 h.h. horse could be given one scoopful three times a day – that is, 4 kg (9 lb) of hard feed per day.

- Each horse has very individual requirements. To formulate a ration, start by following some basic guidelines and then be prepared to make a number of small adjustments until you have a ration to suit your horse's needs.

k.   The grass-kept pony may only need a half scoop three times a day, especially if it is eating larger quantities of hay.

l.   Describe what you would feed in this simple way, and that is all your examiner needs to know. It really is that simple.

Follow-up Work to Confirm Knowledge and Experience

1.   When visiting different yards or trade stands at shows, look at all the different types of feed on offer to help you to become familiar with a wide range of feedstuffs.

2.   Find out about feeding programmes in use with any horses you come across. Compare how different people feed horses of various sizes and types in different types of work. Look at these horses and their performance records to help you to decide if their feed programmes have been well worked out.

Helpful Hints and Exam Technique

In an exam situation candidates often come to grief when describing how much concentrate and hay they will feed a variety of horses. This is mainly caused by not relating what they actually feed to horses on a day-to-day basis to a quantity they can describe in words. It is vital that students practise weighing out quantities of all different types of feed, including hay and haylage. If students only give feeds that have been measured out for them, they may develop a good eye for the right quantity but how will they describe that quantity to their examiner?

Another common mistake is to refer to quantities required by the horse as percentages but then to be unable to work out the mathematics to convert these percentages into actual amounts of feed. Don't use this process if you cannot follow it through! You need to be able to express amounts in pounds or kilograms, it doesn't matter which, so some basic mathematical ability is required. For example, if you think a horse needs 12.7 kg (28 lb) of feed a day and half of that should be hay, then the horse will receive 6.3 kg (14 lb) of hay and 6.3 kg (14 lb) of concentrate. You then need to be able to divide the 6.3 kg (14 lb) of concentrates into three or four feeds. Three feeds of 1.8–2.3 kg (4–5 lb) is accurate enough.

8   Saddlery, Its Use, Care and Fitting

For horse and rider to work safely and in harmony, it is essential to select the right tack for the job in mind, to be able to fit it correctly and to be able to check it is in safe condition for use.

1. Tacking up Procedure

Most tacking up, fastening of buckles, etc., is conducted from the nearside of the horse. In this way, there is less need to keep passing from one side of the horse to the other, which might unsettle it.

The Saddle

a. Either place the numnah separately on the horse's back or attach it to the saddle and then place both saddle and numnah together well forward over the withers (in order to keep the hair lying flat) and slide them back into place just behind the shoulders.

b. The girth may already have been attached on one side and will have been laid over the top of the saddle. It can now be let down, taking care not to let it drop and bang against the horse's legs.

c. Check that the numnah is smooth under the saddle and that it has been lifted well up into the gullet to prevent it from putting pressure on the spine.

d. Do up the girth on the other side. Pull it up gently, not making it too tight too quickly. Most horses tense against the girth as it is done up. When they relax again, the girth becomes loose and will need further adjustment.

e. After checking and tightening the girth, lift each foreleg in turn

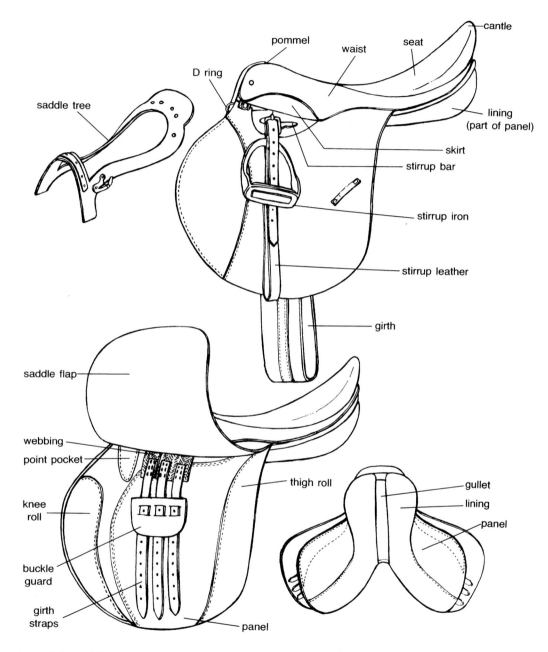

pommel

waist

seat

cantle

D ring

saddle tree

lining
(part of panel)

skirt

stirrup bar

stirrup iron

stirrup leather

girth

saddle flap

webbing

point pocket

thigh roll

gullet

lining

panel

knee
roll

buckle
guard

girth
straps

panel

The points of the saddle

and pull it forward. This action smooths the hair and skin under the girth, so avoiding any pinching.

The Bridle

The horse's head is a very sensitive area. All movements required for putting on the bridle should be gentle, while positive control is maintained.

    a. Untie the horse, place the rope over its neck and remove the head collar. Buckle the head collar around the horse's neck, where it can be used to restrain the horse if it tries to move away.

    b. Check that the throatlatch and noseband have been undone. Hold the bridle in your left hand while you put the reins over the horse's head and place them well back down its neck.

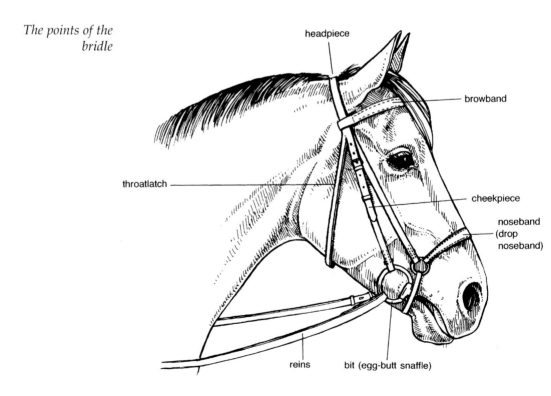

The points of the bridle

headpiece

browband

throatlatch

cheekpiece

noseband (drop noseband)

reins

bit (egg-butt snaffle)

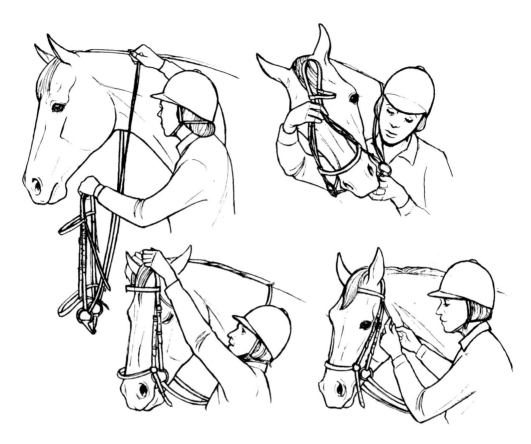

Correct procedure for putting on a bridle

    c. Stand with your right shoulder under the horse's throat and gently slide your right hand around the horse's nose.

    d. Pass the bridle into your right hand, holding it halfway down the cheekpieces, and lift the bit up to the horse's mouth. (This right hand also rests gently on the nose to prevent the horse from raising its head too high.)

    e. With the thumb and first finger of the left hand, push the bit gently into the horse's mouth while you use your two middle fingers to open its mouth. (Your fingers should slide into the mouth in the gap between the two sets of teeth.)

f. Once the bit is in position, keep the bridle lifted with the right hand, to prevent the bit from slipping out again. Take hold of the headpiece with the left hand and gently push the offside ear forward underneath it with the right hand. Push the nearside ear into place in the same way.

g. Check that the forelock and mane are smoothly separated under the headpiece, then secure the throatlatch and noseband.

Accessories

The martingale can be slipped over the horse's head before putting the saddle on. The girth can then be slipped straight through the martingale loop.

2. Fitting the Equipment

GP Saddle

The tree, around which the saddle is built, is made in various widths, usually narrow, medium and wide. Saddles are also made with different lengths of seat to accommodate various sizes of rider. The saddle should be fitted without a numnah then girthed up with the horse standing level.

a. When placed on the horse's back, there must be a clear passage down the gullet. No weight should be taken on the horse's spine.

b. There should be approximately 10 cm (4 in) clearance between the pommel and the withers, without the rider.

c. The saddle should be level, neither too low at the front nor at the back, which would tip the rider forwards or backwards.

d. The full surface of the panels should be in contact with the horse's back. These will distribute the rider's weight over the largest possible area.

e. The length of the saddle should suit the length of the horse's back. There should not be any weight on the loins.

f. The knee roll, panels and saddle flap should not protrude over the shoulder, as they may restrict the horse's freedom of movement.

g. The fitting of the saddle is not complete until seen with the rider on top. The rider's weight will reduce the amount of clearance over the withers and spine.

Snaffle Bridle

Bridles are made in different sizes: pony, cob and full size. There are also different widths and strengths of leather. For example, bridles for heavy-weight horses and hunters will be made of strong, broad strips of leather, while bridles for show ponies will be made from finer leather.

a. The job of the browband is to keep the headpiece from slipping back down the horse's neck. It should not pull the headpiece forward where it will rub, but should keep it in place just behind the ears.

b. The throatlatch, which is attached to the headpiece, has the job of stopping the bridle being pulled off over the horse's ears. It should not be tight when the horse flexes at the poll. When correctly adjusted, you should be able to fit the width of your hand between the horse's cheek and the throatlatch.

c. Apart from having the throatlatch attached to it, the headpiece also supports the cheekpieces.

d. The cheekpieces have the job of supporting the bit and should be long or short enough to enable you to adjust the bit to the correct level.

e. The reins are attached to the bit to give the rider control. They should not be too short, which may cause the rider to let go if the horse suddenly snatches its head down, nor should they be too long which may lead to them becoming tangled around the rider's foot.

f. The job of the cavesson noseband is as a point of attachment for a standing martingale. However, it is often worn just to make the bridle look complete. It should sit the width of two fingers below the projecting cheek bones and be loose around the nose to allow free movement of the jaws. Allow for the width of two fingers between the front of the horse's nose and the noseband.

g. The snaffle bit should be adjusted to a height where it wrinkles the corners of the horse's mouth. The mouthpiece should not protrude more than 6 mm ($^1/_4$ in) on either side of the horse's mouth, nor should the bit rings appear to pinch inwards. If the bit is too wide, it will slide from side to side when the rider uses the reins. If it is too narrow, it will pinch and rub the sides of the mouth.

Martingales

a. The neck straps of both the standing and running martingale should fit around the base of the neck, allowing for the width of one hand to be placed between the neck and the neck strap.

b. To fit the standing martingale, place the neck strap over the horse's head and attach one end to the girth. Then follow the line of the underside of the horse's neck with the martingale strap, up under its throat and down to its chin groove.

c. To fit the running martingale, place the strap over the horse's neck and attach the end to the girth. If both rings are drawn back along the line of the shoulder, they should be approximately 15–20 cm (6–8 in) short of reaching the withers.

d. Rein stops must be worn with the running martingale. They will prevent the rings from becoming stuck where the reins buckle on to the bit.

Martingales fitted

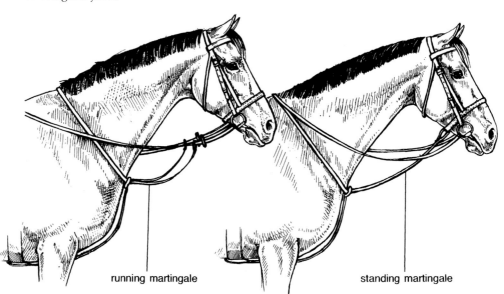

running martingale   standing martingale

e. Both martingales have the job of preventing the horse from raising its head too high: the standing type by exerting pressure on the nose via the cavesson noseband; the running type by exerting pressure on the reins, which is then transferred to the bit.

f. The running martingale will only work if the rider has a contact on the reins.

g. Provided they are correctly adjusted, both types of martingale should allow the horse free movement of the head and neck while working on the flat or over fences. They should only come into action when the horse tries to raise its head too high for the rider to maintain control.

3. Care of the Equipment

The Thorough Cleaning Process

a. Undo all the buckles and take the tack completely apart. This includes removing stirrups and leathers, girth, numnah, reins, bit, cheekpieces, etc.

b. The bit, stirrups and treads can be washed in warm water then dried.

c. Remove any grease on the leather. This can be done with a blunt knife if care is taken not to scratch the leather.

d. Using lukewarm water, make a sponge damp, not wet, and work it over all the leather until it is clean.

e. Next, use a damp sponge to apply a layer of saddle soap which should be worked well into the leather.

f. A matchstick or tooth pick makes a useful instrument with which to clean all the buckle holes that have become clogged with grease or soap.

g. The stirrups and other metalwork can be cleaned with metal polish. Do not apply metal polish to the bit.

h. Girths and numnahs made of washable fabric can usually be hand or machine washed.

i. Synthetic saddles are washed using a stiff brush and lukewarm water then left to dry.

j. This complete cleaning process should take place after the tack has been used a maximum of five to six times. For horses in regular work, this is usually once a week.

After Each Use

a. Always wash the bit to prevent an accumulation of dried saliva and food which would soon rub the horse's mouth.
b. Remove the girth and numnah, brush clean and leave to air.
c. If boots are worn, brush or wash clean and leave to air.
d. Slip the bridle straps out of their keepers and run down the stirrups. With a damp sponge, remove obvious grease, mud and sweat. Work in a layer of saddle soap.

Additional Points on Cleaning and Care

a. While cleaning the tack, keep a constant check on its condition and therefore its safety.
b. If the tack gets very wet, take it apart and leave it to dry. Clean with a damp sponge then apply a layer of leather dressing. This will replace the oil lost and make the leather more supple. When the dressing has soaked in, apply a layer of saddle soap.
c. New leather will become more supple if leather dressing is applied. All leather will benefit from an application of dressing three or four times a year.
d. Tack should be kept in a warm room. If the atmosphere is damp, the leather will become mouldy and will rot but if it is too warm and dry the leather will dry out and crack.

Checking the Tack for Safety

a. All of the stitching will weaken and rot eventually. At the first signs of weakness, the item concerned should be sent to the saddler for restitching.
b. On the saddle, keep a particularly close check on the stitching that attaches the girth straps to the webbing under the saddle flaps. It undergoes considerable strain and if it rots your girth will no longer be secure!
c. The stitching that secures the buckle of the stirrup leather also takes a lot of strain, as does the stitching on the girth. Check these each time you use them.

d. The girth straps are often stitched to two separate pieces of webbing. If your girth is buckled to the first strap (attached to the first webbing) and either of the second two straps (attached to the second webbing), you have more security should one webbing break. Check the webbing for signs of wear.

> • On the saddle, keep a particularly close check on the stitching that attaches the girth straps to the webbing under the saddle flap

e. The vital areas on the bridle include the stitching at the buckle and bit ends of the reins and on the cheekpieces.

f. Another major area of wear occurs at all buckle holes. These sometimes stretch so much that one hole begins to run into another. This severely weakens the leather which will then break easily. This frequently occurs on the girth straps.

g. Where straps are always buckled in the same hole, the leather may begin to crack from being constantly bent.

4. Injuries from Dirty or Ill-fitting Tack

If tack is dirty or does not fit correctly, it will rub, causing galls and bruising. The most common sites of these injuries are:

- the girth area just behind the elbow
- on top of and on either side of the withers
- either side of the spine just under the back of the saddle
- behind the ears
- just under the projecting cheek bones
- the corners of the horse's mouth
- the chin groove

Treatment

a. Find and remove the cause.
b. Treat as a minor wound.

Tacked up and ready to ride

c. There are various ways in which the horse can be exercised while the wound is healing. Try ride and lead, use a bitless bridle or lunge.

Follow-up Work to Confirm Knowledge and Experience

1. There is no substitute for hands-on experience. Practise tacking up as many different horses and ponies as possible and check the fitting of tack in order to develop a good eye for fit.

Helpful Hints and Exam Technique

 At Stage One, candidates shouldn't worry if they come across an item of tack they are not familiar with. As long as they can make a sensible assessment of the item and work out what it is, the examiner will be happy, not expecting candidates at this level to have experience of every item. Candidates should, however, be familiar with items in common usage.

 A good way of keeping up to date with new items on the market is to visit the local saddlery shop and have a good look at all the items on offer.

 Before starting on a task set, have a good look at the horse you are working with to see if it is likely to need a narrow saddle or a small bridle, for example.

 A common mistake made by candidates is not checking both sides of the equipment once they have fitted it to the horse. For example, they may put on a bridle and not realise that the noseband is sitting much higher on one side than the other, or that the cheekpieces are not adjusted to the same height on each side.

 Always adjust tack to fit the horse. Candidates often put an item on, then tell the examiner it doesn't fit. If there are adjustment holes available, the examiner will then ask the candidate to adjust the item to fit. The candidate would give a much better impression if they had made these adjustments without being prompted.

9   Horse Clothing

The horse will benefit if the right clothing is selected for the occasion, and is correctly fitted and well cared for.

1. Rugs

Many different fastenings, materials and designs are used for every possible occasion. To check your horse's rug size, measure from the middle of its chest right around along its side to the point of the buttock. The rug is measured in a similar way: laid flat on the floor and measured from chest strap to the end of the rug.

To Rug Up

a. When putting the rug on, avoid throwing it over the horse, which may startle it, and aim to keep its hair lying flat. At the same time, take care to fold leg or surcingle straps over the rug to prevent them from swinging against the horse's legs and causing injury.

b. Fold the rug in half by bringing the tail end forward towards the wither end. Then place the folded rug well forward over the horse's withers. Unfold the rug and slide it back into place. It is best to leave it a little too far forward, as it will tend to slip back once the horse begins to move.

c. In general, it is best to fasten the roller or surcingles before the front straps. Some horses bite at the front of their rugs while the roller is being fastened and if the front strap is already buckled the horse could get its lower jaw caught in the front of the rug. Likewise, if the front strap is fastened first on a breezy day, the rug may blow forward and become tangled around the horse's front legs.

Rugging up using an underblanket

d. For the same reasons, undo the front strap first when removing the rug (and leg straps if used).

e. As there are many variations of surcingles and fastenings in current use, each person will need to assess the individual situation and secure the fastenings in whichever order seems most appropriate at the time.

f. If a roller is used to secure the rug, it needs to be firmly buckled to stop the rug from slipping. To prevent undue pressure, there should be plenty of padding between the horse's withers and the roller.

g. Cross-over surcingles incorporated into the rug avoid the pressure problems that rollers can cause and are favoured by many owners. The design is an excellent contribution to the comfort of the horse. They should be adjusted to hang just 3–5 cm (1–2 in) below the horse's belly. This type of rug is usually darted and shaped to fit the contours of the horse's body more closely. This helps to prevent slipping.

Sheet with cross surcingles

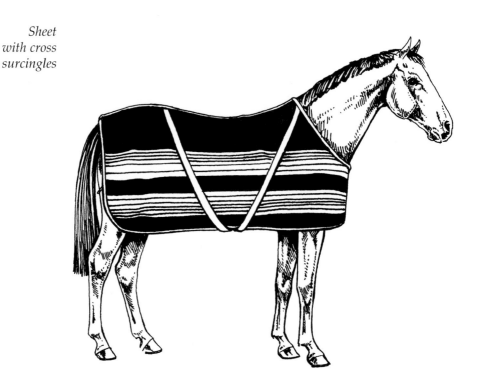

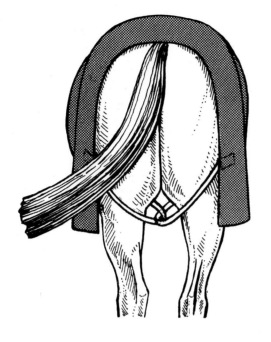

h. As horses are more active in the field, most turn-out rugs (New Zealands) have leg straps to help secure them. These should be adjusted to allow freedom of movement and should hang down approximately level with the inner aspect of the second thigh. Fasten one leg strap, then link the other strap through the first one before fastening. The two straps are thus linked together which aids the stability of the rug and prevents rubbing.

i. Blankets are less popular now that fitted under-rugs, made from various materials, are available. If a blanket is used, fold it in half and lay it over the horse, well forward on its neck. Unfold it and slide it back into place. Take each of the front corners in turn and fold them back towards the withers, leaving a triangular section of blanket pointing forward up the horse's neck. Place the rug on top, then fold the triangular section of blanket back over the top of the rug. It may reach far enough back to be secured under the roller but this really depends on how large the blanket is. Fasten the rug in the usual way.

New Zealand rug, used for horses turned out in the field

j. When removing rugs, undo leg straps, front straps and rollers or surcingles. Fold any trailing straps over the rug then fold the rug in half by bringing the wither end back towards the tail end. Slide the rug back and off, leaving the horse's hair lying flat.

Further Points

a. All types of rug should be secured with a roller, surcingle, cross surcingles or legs straps. This is sometimes forgotten when sweat or summer sheets are used as they are not always made with surcingles attached.

b. Some turn-out rugs are made extra deep at the sides for warmth and protection from the weather.

c. Some rugs may be fitted with a fillet string. This is a piece of cord attached to the two back corners of the rug, which hangs level with the second thigh and fits around the back of the horse's legs under its tail. The fillet string is used to prevent the back of the rug from blowing out and up in breezy conditions. It is particularly useful on light rugs that may be worn outside at shows or when travelling.

Another style of turnout rug, with cross surcingles and a tail flap. The rug is made from a strong, waterproof, modern material

d. Rugs should fit snugly around the base of the horse's neck. If the front section hangs low on the chest, the rug will slip back too easily and rub the horse's shoulders. If the length is correct, the rug should reach the top of the horse's tail. If it is much longer or shorter than this, the shaped parts of the rug will not correspond with the shape of the horse.

e. Most rugs will be labelled with washing or cleaning instructions. Those made of washable material may fit in your washing machine, making cleaning easy. (Not all domestic machines are large enough to cope with a large rug.) Waxed or waterproof rugs will need to be brushed clean and may need rewaxing or reproofing to keep them waterproof. Some companies specialise in rug cleaning and repair. Your saddler will probably know if there is a rug cleaner in your area.

f. How frequently your rugs are washed or cleaned depends entirely upon how much they are worn. A stable rug in constant use will probably need washing every two to four weeks, while a turn-out rug may need brushing off regularly and then be cleaned only once a year. Any leather work on your rugs should be oiled and saddle soaped as frequently as your other tack.

g. When not in use, rugs should be stored on shelves or hangers in a dry atmosphere. Take precautions against moths and vermin which can easily ruin an expensive rug.

h. Some rugs have woollen linings. These may irritate a horse with sensitive skin, especially if it has been clipped. Other horses may be too warm in a thick, quilted rug, or may fit one particular design of rug better than another. All these factors, and others such as cost, need to be considered when choosing a rug.

- All equipment should be cleaned regularly. Some, like bandages, light stable rugs and numnahs, can go in the washing machine.

i. The type of sweat rug that resembles a string vest should always be used in conjunction with a second rug. Used on its own, it has no purpose. The idea is for it to trap a layer of air between the horse and the outer rug. This layer of air circulates and helps to dry a wet horse without letting it become chilled.

j. Sweat sheets or coolers come into their own for horses returning hot and sweaty from competition. There are some very good modern designs which draw away moisture from the horse's coat and out to the outer surface of the rug where it evaporates away thus keeping the horse warm while it dries and preventing chills. They are usually fitted with cross surcingles or belly strap and fillet string, which does away with the need for rollers. It must be uncomfortable for the horse to have a firmly fitted roller put around its middle when it has just been relieved of the girth which was holding the saddle on. These modern sheets can also double as summer sheets or travelling rugs, which obviously cuts down on costs.

- Rugs should fit snugly around the base of the horse's neck. If the front section hangs low on the chest, the rug will slip back easily and rub the horse's shoulders

k. Even on a warm day, it is a good idea to put a cooler/sweat sheet on the horse after a competition. While cooling off and drying, the tired horse can easily begin to feel cold. However, it is also necessary to make sure you don't over-rug and thus distress the horse by making it too warm.

2. Tail Bandages

a. Tail bandages are a little less stretchy than exercise bandages but are made from similar material, approximately 7–8 cm (2³/₄–2 in) wide, with cotton ties.

b. They are used to protect the tail while travelling and to help to improve the horse's appearance by keeping the top of the tail smooth, especially after it has been pulled.

c. A tail bandage should not be left on for more than one hour. As it has to be applied firmly to prevent it from slipping down, it

Shape the tail after bandaging

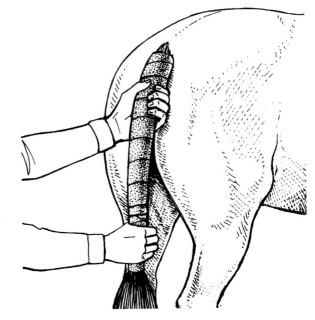

could interfere with circulation if left on too long. This may cause the hair to fall out!

d. Damp the tail hair at the top of the tail before applying the bandage. This aids grip for the first few turns.

e. For even pressure, keep the bandage smooth and overlap each turn evenly, as well as keeping the tension of the tapes, when tied, the same as the bandage.

f. Bandage almost to the end of the dock for a pleasing appearance and a firm base to work around.

g. When travelling, finish the bandage by winding it a few centimetres back up the tail, tie the tapes slightly to one side, and fold the last turn of your bandage down over the tapes to cover them. This helps to prevent them being rubbed undone if the horse leans its tail against the wall in the box. If the bandage is finished and tied too high, the tapes and knot may rub against the horse and cause a sore.

h. Finally, with one hand under the tail, reshape it to follow the contour of the horse's hindquarters so that the horse is not left with its tail sticking out at an uncomfortable angle.

i. To remove the bandage, untie the tapes then slide the whole bandage off in one piece, from the top, down the horse's tail.

Follow-up Work to Confirm Knowledge and Experience

1. It is advisable to practise putting on, checking the fitting and taking off as great a range of equipment as possible. As already mentioned, as so many different designs are now available, confidence will improve if the candidate is familiar with a wide range of designs. Visiting the local saddlery shop is helpful in this.
2. Speed and efficiency are important qualities to develop. A good way to do this is to be involved with horses going to competitions. Having to prepare horses for travelling, which must be ready for a certain deadline, or take care of a horse as it completes its competition, are good ways of improving these qualities.

Helpful Hints and Exam Technique

Check the available equipment carefully before you select what you are going to use for the task set. In an exam situation it is easy to miss something. Although you will be expected to be quick and efficient, it will be easier for you to do a good job if you have selected the right items to start with.

In your place of work, practise talking about the equipment you are fitting while you are fitting it. Although you do not have to talk while you work in the exam, there may be something you would like to point out to the examiner while they are observing your work. Practising this skill will help you to put over more information as you go along. However, you should remember that the ability to perform the practical skill is the most important part of the practical sections, rather than an ability to talk about it.

10 Shoeing

1. The External Structure of the Foot

a. The outer wall of the hoof is hard and insensitive. Divided into toe, quarters and heels, it doesn't quite form a circle because it turns inwards at the heels to form the bars. This allows for expansion and provides extra strength at the heels. The wall is made of horn which contains many tubules that grow down from the top to the bottom of the wall.

b. The coronet band forms the junction between the lower limb and the wall.

c. From just above the coronet grows the periople. This is a thin layer of skin that grows down over the wall and controls evaporation of moisture from the horn.

d. Most of the ground surface of the foot consists of the sole which is concave to the ground.

e. The white line can be seen between the edge of the sole and the wall. This is the visible part of the horny laminae.

f. The area of sole between the wall and the bars is called the seat of corn.

g. The rest of the ground surface is occupied by the frog. This is wedge-shaped, formed from soft, elastic horn and has a central cleft. It aids grip and helps to absorb concussion.

h. At the rear of the hoof are the bulbs of the heels.

2. Recognising the Need for Reshoeing

Most horses need reshoeing every four to six weeks. This will depend upon how much road/hard ground work the horse does, how quickly the hoof grows and whether the shoe becomes twisted, loose, lost, etc.

a. Part or all of the shoe has worn thin, resulting in less grip. This can be dangerous, especially when riding on the road.

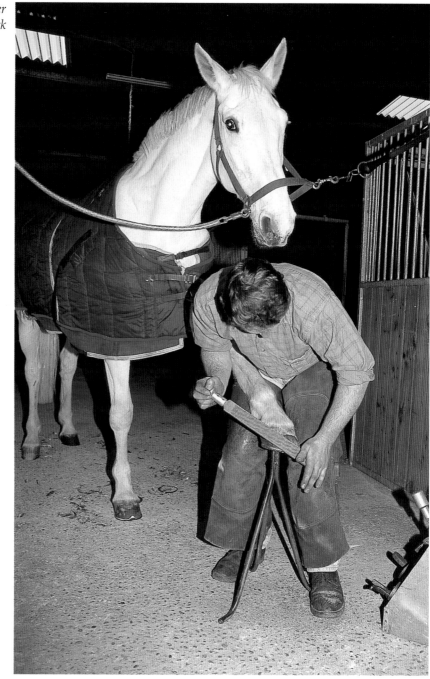

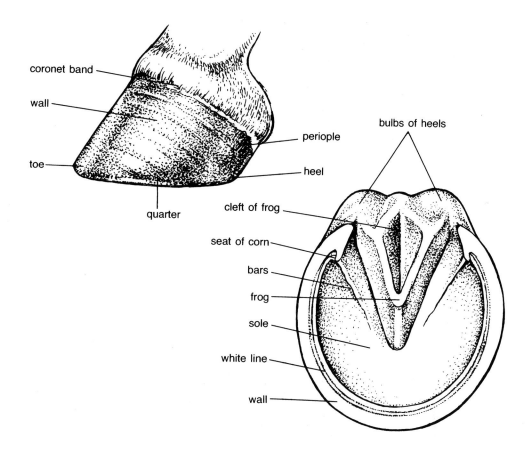

coronet band

wall

toe

quarter

periople

heel

bulbs of heels

cleft of frog

seat of corn

bars

frog

sole

white line

wall

The external structure of the foot

    b. A loose shoe may twist off at any time. The cast shoe may then be trodden on by the horse, causing a nail to puncture its sole.

    c. Risen clenches – The shoe will soon be loose and a risen clench can cause damage if the horse brushes.

    d. Long feet – If the foot looks long at the toe, pick it up and examine the heel area. Excess growth will have moved the shoe forward, causing the foot to grow over the shoe at the heels. This can push the heels of the shoe into the seat of corn, resulting in bruising and lameness.

Long foot, with risen clenches, in need of reshoeing

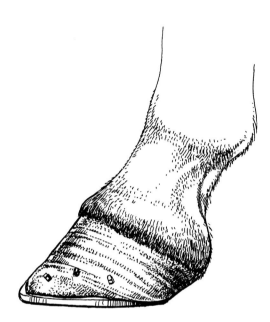

e. The horse may have cast a shoe. In this case check that all the nails have been removed from the wall.

f. Twisted shoe – Due to the shoe being trodden on by another horse, or by the horse treading on a front shoe with a hind foot, it may be twisted. This could lead to lameness.

g. Cracked and broken feet – Horses with brittle feet may lose chunks of horn. This is likely to loosen the shoe.

If a horse's shoes are hardly worn, the farrier may reshoe the horse with the same set of shoes. This process is called a remove.

Follow-up Work to Confirm Knowledge and Experience

1. Watch the farrier at work whenever possible, especially when different horses are being shod and if different shoes are being used. Make sure you know and understand each stage of the process.

2. Study the different tools available for use by the farrier to make sure you can recognise each one.

Horse's hoof in need of reshoeing; there is evidence of risen clenches, broken hoof and worn shoe

A well-shod hoof

Helpful Hints and Exam Technique

Carry a hoof pick in your pocket. When talking about shoeing and the horse's shoes, you will find it easier to take out your own hoof pick to pick out feet and examine the shoes rather than having to go in search of one. Don't forget to pick out feet into a skip to keep the yard and bed clean.

11 Health

1. Signs of the Horse being in Good Health

a. The horse should be "well covered" or "well furnished"; that is, enough muscle and fat on its body to cover its skeletal frame in such a way that there are no prominent bony areas.

b. The horse is alert, with ears mobile.

c. It is eating and drinking normally.

d. Salmon-pink mucous membranes.

e. Supple skin, moving easily over the body.

f. A shine to the coat.

g. No abnormal heat or swellings.

h. When a skin recoil test is made (that is, the skin on the neck is pinched between thumb and first finger), the skin should recoil immediately, demonstrating its elasticity.

i. Droppings should break as they hit the ground, and be green or golden in colour depending upon the feed eaten. Horses pass droppings approximately ten to 15 times during a 24-hour period, depending upon the diet fed.

j. Urine should be pale yellow.

k. Normal temperature: 100–101°F or 38°C at rest.

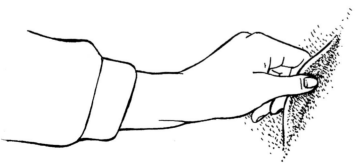

Neck pinch, used in a skin recoil test. The test is for signs of dehydration in the horse

A horse in excellent health. Note the alert expression, shiny coat and the well-furnished body. There are no obvious signs of ailment or injury

l. Normal pulse 35–45 beats per minute; higher for foals, varying between 50–100 beats per minute at rest.
m. Normal respiration: 8–12 in-and-out breaths per minute at rest.
n. Able to carry its weight evenly on all four feet.
o. No sign of discharge from nose or eyes. Eyes fully open.
p. Normal response to capillary refill test. This is tested by pressing the horse's gum with your thumb, which restricts the flow of

blood. When you remove your thumb, the capillaries should immediately refill with blood.

2. Signs of the Horse being Unwell

a. If any one, or all of these, is prominent: ribs/hips/croup/back-bone, or if the top of the neck is sunken, then the horse is underweight.
b. Not alert, head low and ears unresponsive.
c. Not eating or drinking usual amounts.
d. Mucous membranes may be yellow (indicating jaundice and disruption of the liver), pale (indicating anaemia, probably due to infection) or blue (indicating lack of oxygen, due to poor circulation).
e. Skin appears taut. When the skin recoil test is made, the pinched skin stands proud, being slow to recoil.
f. The coat is dull and staring.
g. Abnormal areas of heat and swelling.
h. Droppings may be loose, very hard and/or irregular.
i. Urine red/brown or black.
j. TPR may be raised or lowered: temperature more than 1°F, or 0.5°C above or below normal. Pulse raised or lowered. Respiration shallow and rapid.
k. Showing unlevel steps.
l. Discharge from the nostrils or eyes.
m. Eyes not fully open and/or third eye lid showing.
n. Blood slow to return to capillaries after refill test.
o. Showing signs of discomfort. For example, pacing round the box, looking around at, or kicking at, belly; frequently getting up and lying down; pawing the ground; trying to stale and failing; patchy sweat; "tucked up".
p. Excessively overweight.

• In order to keep track of vet visits, shoeing, dentistry, and worming and vaccination dates, individual records should be kept for each horse.

Finally, as individual horses have their own distinct behaviour patterns and habits, make sure that you know your own horse well. In this way you will notice the slightest abnormality that may indicate ill health. Act immediately if you notice something is amiss. Report to the yard manager or call the vet. Quick responses may limit the spread of any disease, reduce the need for lengthy treatment and keep the horse's suffering to a minimum.

Follow-up Work to Confirm Knowledge and Experience

1. To gain experience in all matters to do with the horse's health, it is essential to have worked with a large number of horses and ponies. Until you have actually seen a variety of diseases/wounds and have been involved in treating and nursing these horses, you cannot be completely aware of the problems involved and the signs to look for.

Helpful Hints and Exam Technique

Some candidates make the mistake of forgetting the obvious when asked about the horse's health. The examiner is usually looking for basic practical answers not complicated veterinary knowledge, which is best left to the vets themselves.

12 Safety When Working and Riding

1. Safety

Clothing for Working around Horses

a. Strong footwear, to protect you if trodden on, etc., is essential. The ideal would be boots with steel toe caps which are now more readily available. Leather boots give good protection. The soles must provide good grip.

b. All clothing must allow freedom of movement. However, if too loose and baggy, it can catch on things or flap and frighten the horse.

c. Bright colours may be frightening. If worn, the wearer should be aware of introducing them gradually to their horses.

d. Gloves should be worn whenever possible. By preventing wounds and scratches on your hands, you avoid problems like tetanus and Weil's disease.

e. All jewellery should be avoided. Rings, bracelets, earrings, etc., can easily get caught up and cause serious injury to the wearer.

f. Long hair can also get caught and is better tied back or worn under a hat.

- A yard tidy and free from debris will help to reduce the risk of accidents. Unswept areas left littered with hay and straw will increase the risk of fire spreading, implements with sharp prongs can injure horses if stepped upon, and items like haynets and forks become dangerous hazards if left where they may cause people to trip up.

g. A hard hat should be worn when handling problem or young horses.

h. For riding, a hard hat of Standard PAS 015 or EN1384 must always be worn. Footwear must have a small block heel, not a wedge type, to prevent the foot from slipping through the stirrup and becoming stuck. The sole should be fairly smooth, as deep ridges may also cause feet to get stuck.

General Safety around the Yard

Keeping the yard tidy is the most important step towards safety. Any item left lying around can become a hazard. The tidying up process is usually called "setting fair".

Procedure for tying up a hay net

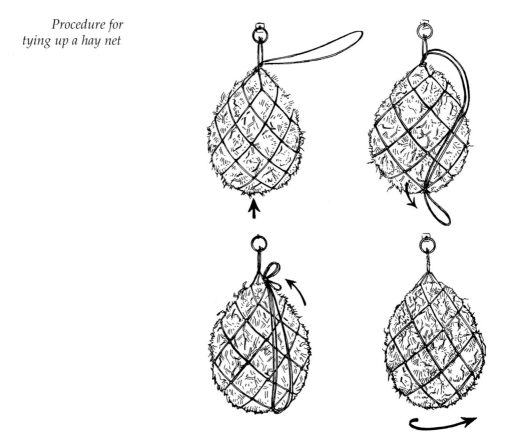

a. Grooming kit, tack, clothing, buckets, etc., must always be put away. Hay nets pose a particular hazard for both horse and human if left lying around.

b. When a full hay net is given to a horse, it should be tied up bearing in mind how low it will hang when empty. Pull the hay net up as high as possible, then draw the string through the bottom of the hay net and pull it back up to the top. Tie with a quick-release knot, then turn the net so that the knot is hidden at the back where it is less likely to be pulled undone by the horse.

c. Yard work often involves moving heavy objects. This can be hazardous if not tackled correctly. Always enlist the help of a fellow worker where possible. Trolleys, wheelbarrows, etc., should be used to move hay bales, feed sacks and other items, rather than trying to carry them.

d. When lifting, try to keep your back straight. Bend your knees rather than bending at the waist and push up using your thigh muscles, rather than pulling up with your back muscles.

e. Keep weights balanced; for example, carry two water buckets,

Lifting a heavy weight; the incorrect way (left) and the correct way (right)

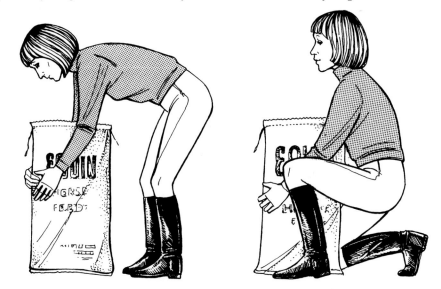

one in each hand, rather than one on its own which will pull you sideways.

f. Carry heavy weights close to your body to help you to maintain balance.

g. General maintenance is essential. For example, door bolts need to work smoothly; electrical fittings must be secure and well insulated; holes in the yard or buildings need quick repair, and so on.

h. A bag or bin can be provided for any string removed from hay and straw bales.

i. Yard tools require hooks to hang them from or a specific room where they can be stored.

j. The yard surface should be non-slip and kept free from debris by regular sweeping. This will also remove loose hay and straw that could become a fire hazard.

Further Points on Safety for Winter Weather Conditions

a. Do not empty water buckets, or run a hose, directly on to the yard as the water may freeze and cause a hazardous surface.

b. Grit or salt can be spread over icy patches to maintain a safe surface.

c. Check drains and gutters more frequently as any blockage will quickly cause flooding in very wet weather.

d. Automatic water systems may need to be switched off and drained to prevent freezing and subsequent burst pipes.

e. Be aware that stabled horses often become more lively and difficult to handle in cold, windy weather. It may be necessary to lead a horse in its bridle for more control, even though you may normally lead it out on its head collar.

f. When riding out, be aware of slippery surfaces and previously muddy ground frozen into hard ruts. These hazardous surfaces may cause a fall and injury if not tackled with extra care.

g. Check field water troughs several times a day to break ice. Some self-filling troughs may not refill if pipes freeze, so check the water level.

h. Shorter, dark days mean that you frequently have to work in the dark, while power cuts are more likely in stormy weather. Try to prioritise and carry out essential jobs in the daylight. Make sure you know where to locate the trip switches, and keep plenty of torches to hand.

Fire Precautions

a. Prevention is best so keep the yard tidy (as mentioned above) to prevent the spread of fire if it occurs.
b. A muck heap can get very hot and may self-ignite, so position it well away from buildings.
c. Hay, straw and shavings should be stored away from the stables.
d. Taps, hoses and troughs (keep them full) can all be used to fight a fire.
e. Arrange for a fire officer to visit. He or she will advise on fire extinguishers, telling you how many are needed, where to put them and what type to have.
f. Put up one or more fire notices. These should have white lettering on a green background and read as follows:

IN THE EVENT OF A FIRE
1. Raise the alarm.
2. Move horses to safety.
3. Dial 999 for the fire brigade.
4. Fight the fire.

After each point, details are required:

- The location of the fire alarm.
- Designated place of safety for the horses.
- Location of the nearest telephone.
- Location of fire fighting equipment.

g. Put NO SMOKING notices around the yard and provide buckets full of sand in which cigarettes can be extinguished.
h. All workers should know and practise the yard fire drill.

Riding Out and the Country Code

There are various rules of safe conduct which help to maintain a good relationship between riders and other countryside users.

a. If on horseback when passing walkers or other riders, always walk and give them a wide berth. If you approach them from the rear, make your presence known. It is, in any case, only polite to say "Good morning", etc.
b. Do not ride on private land without permission. Keep to bridleways and other areas designated for horses.
c. Ride around the edges of fields with crops in them.
d. Do not ride through livestock. Walk around them, giving them a wide berth.
e. Leave gates as you find them, unless it is obvious that someone has forgotten to secure a gate and livestock are escaping, in which case inform the farmer.
f. Be aware of people, dogs, etc., in gardens. When hidden from your horse's view, behind a hedge or fence, any noise or movement could cause your horse to shy into the road.
g. Never trot around blind corners on roads or tracks. There could be any number of unforeseen hazards, so be prepared and slow to a walk.
h. Avoid busy roads where possible, and take the Riding and Road Safety Test.

2. Accident Procedure and Reports

It is advisable for everyone to have first-aid training, whatever their occupation. The following is the procedure to take in the event of an accident, rather than how to administer first aid.

Accident Procedure

a. First, remain calm as it is important to think clearly.
b. While the injured person is your first priority, you must make the situation safe while you make your way to them. If someone has been kicked, move the horse away. If someone has fallen off, halt the rest of the ride and send a responsible person to catch the loose horse. Each situation will be a little different, so use common sense.

c. Go to the injured person. Reassure them and tell them to keep still.

If Conscious

d. Encourage them to breathe deeply and calmly. (They may be winded and panicking about getting air.)
e. Ask them if there is any pain. Can they move their fingers and toes?
f. Make a mental note of what they say; it will be helpful information to give the doctor or ambulance staff, should they be needed.
g. Keep talking to the person. If they appear to be talking nonsense, they may have concussion and will need to be taken to a doctor.
h. If they cannot move their fingers or toes or have pain in the neck, back or limbs, do not move them. Ask for an ambulance to be called. Keep them warm with a blanket or jackets. Do not try to remove hat or boots, etc.
i. Obvious bleeding should be stemmed by applying direct pressure with a handkerchief or clean pad.
j. If they feel fine and want to get up, allow them to do so on their own. Stand near in case they feel faint and need support. Do not allow them to remount if you feel there is any chance they may faint, or if they have hit their head.
k. Allow them to walk for a while before remounting, and continue with an easy, confidence-giving exercise, or let them sit quietly before resuming their work which should be of an undemanding nature.

- If an accident involves injury to human and horse, take care of the human first, but make sure the horse is attended to as soon as possible

If Unconscious

l. Check that there is no blockage in the mouth that may prevent breathing and carefully loosen any tight clothing around the neck.

m. Do not move the person unless they are in danger of choking and need their airway kept clear by putting them in the recovery position (this should be done with great care to keep the spine straight). Send for an ambulance. Anyone who has been unconscious must be examined by a doctor in case of skull damage.

n. Keep talking to them; this may help to bring them round. Keep them warm.

o. Remain calm and also reassure the rest of your ride as soon as possible. Once the injured person has been taken to hospital, you may resume the work, hack or lesson.

Further Points

a. Be prepared for accidents. Have the telephone number of your local doctor and vet clearly displayed by the telephone. Dial 999 for an ambulance. Have a human first-aid kit on the yard and also one that can be taken out when hacking.

b. If you have a pay phone, keep money for emergencies in an obvious place beside the phone. When hacking, take money for the phone.

c. If an accident occurs on the road, someone should be posted on each side of an injured person to redirect traffic around them. With luck, there will be a motorist with a mobile phone or you may have a mobile phone with you with which to summon help. It is obviously important to catch the loose horse as it may cause further accidents. On return home you should fill in a British Horse Society accident report form. This helps the Road Safety Development Officer of the BHS to compile statistics on road accidents involving horses.

d. If an accident involves injury to human and horse, take care of the human first but attend to the horse or send someone else to do so as soon as possible.

Accident and Incident Reports

a. In all yards an accident book should be kept in which all incidents and accidents are recorded. You could have two books, one for minor incidents and one for more serious accidents.

b. Records should include: date, place and time of incident, name of person or persons involved and what they were doing at the time, what happened, what injuries (if any) were sustained, what horses (if any) were involved, whether the person was taken to hospital/doctor/home, etc. It is also a good idea to draw a sketch of the incident. For example, the position of jumps and other riders when a person fell off during a lesson.

c. When possible, any one who has witnessed an accident should be asked to sign the report.

d. The accident book should be available for staff and clients to look at if they wish and should therefore be kept in an accessible place in the office or similar room.

3. Knowledge of the British Horse Society (BHS)

As all candidates for the BHS examinations must be BHS members, it is important to understand the aims and objectives of the society, along with how it benefits them and others (not just examination candidates) to be a member.

a. The BHS is a registered animal welfare charity.

b. It aims to improve the quality of life of all horses.

c. It tries to reach these aims by promoting the interests of horse and pony breeding and encouraging the use and protection of horses and ponies. It also makes available, to its members and the general public, information on all aspects of equestrianism.

Follow-up Work to Confirm Knowledge and Experience

1. Through working in an equestrian establishment, it should be possible for any student to observe how important safe working procedures are. Unfortunately, accidents will happen but it is hoped that each individual will learn by their mistakes.

2. Students at all levels need to train themselves to ask the questions "Why?", "How?", "What is it?" and so on, about everything that goes on around them. In this way they will learn

more and have a much deeper understanding of all aspects of yard work and management.

Helpful Hints and Exam Technique

 The subjects of safety, accident procedure and knowledge of the BHS will be examined at all levels. Candidates must show a really thorough knowledge of safety and accident procedure if an examiner is going to have confidence in their ability to work safely and sensibly with horses. While the candidate is unlikely to fail an exam due to lack of knowledge of the BHS, it does not give a very good impression if a person is a member of a society about which they know nothing! For your own sake, read the members' yearbook and see what you can gain from the BHS, rather than just being a member for the sake of your exams.

13 Preparing to Take the Exam

1. Location

a. Once you know where you will be taking the exam it is a good idea to make a visit to the centre if it is not where you are already training.

b. By making a visit you can check your route and find out how long it will take you to get there.

c. On arrival introduce yourself and you will probably find someone only too happy to show you round.

d. You are bound to feel more confident if you know where you are going and what you will find when you arrive.

e. You can also explore local facilities for lunch, or make plans to take sandwiches and drinks with you.

f. Do try to arrange for someone to go with you for the day. It is not a good idea to drive yourself when your mind is occupied with thoughts of the exam.

- By making a visit you can check your route, calculate how long the journey will take, and find the exam location. This should help to reduce some of the stress on the day of the exam.

2. Clothing

a. Smart and practical turn out will immediately make a good impression. For the "Horse Knowledge and Care" section of the exam you need to feel comfortable and able to work easily around the horses.

b. Have your hair tied back if it is long. Wearing a cap is quite acceptable if you feel comfortable doing so, but it is not essential.

c. You will probably be wearing a shirt and tie for the riding section of the exam. Cover this with a plain sweatshirt or jumper in cold weather, or just wear shirt and tie if very warm weather. On colder and wet days a waterproof coat that is not too big and bulky is acceptable.

d. Jodhpurs are easy to work in and should be cream or beige if you are taking the riding section of the exam. If you are only taking the "Horse Knowledge and Care" section you could wear dark-coloured jodhpurs.

Clothed for the exam: (left) *for riding; and* (centre and right) *for stable management*

This photograph was taken under examination conditions at The Talland School of Equitation

e. Good strong footwear is essential. Long riding boots can be restrictive to work in, but are perfectly acceptable   if you are comfortable in them. Otherwise jodhpur boots are a smart and practical alternative. Make sure your boots are clean.

f. Take gloves with you for leading horses out of the stable.

- A smart and practical turnout will immediately make a good impression on the examiners. Try to be enthusiastic and keep smiling!

3. Performance

a. Remember that examiners are watching you all the time. They are not just looking to see how you carry out the task set. They are looking at your general attitude to your work and the horses. Do you go about your work quickly? Are you confident and caring with the horses? Do you work in a tidy manner; skip up as you go along, and keep equipment organised?

b. The general impression you make will go a long way towards making the final result a positive one. So try to be helpful and enthusiastic.

c. It is important to be physically as fit as you can be when working with horses. If you work with horses on a daily basis, mucking out, sweeping yards, etc., and pay attention to correct lifting techniques and working procedures you will keep yourself fit and be able to perform to a higher standard both when riding and carrying out yard tasks.

If you are well prepared for this exam and don't rush into it you should find that you enjoy the day. Good luck.

Index

Note: page numbers in *italics* refer to illustrations

accident procedure 118–21
   conscious person 119
   unconscious person 119–20
accident reports 118–21
aggressive behaviour 47, 48, *50*, 51
approaching horse 2, 16, 17–18

barley 72, *74*, 75, *77*
bedding
   systems 35
   types 35–6, *37*
bit 83, 84, 85, 86, 88
boxwalking 54
bran 73, *77*
bridle
   points of *82*
   safety checks 83–4, 88
   snaffle 85–6
   tacking up 80–4
British Horse Society ix, 121, 122
   examination system *x*
   Road Safety Development Officer 120
brushes 24, *25*, *26*, 27, 28–9, 31
bucking 57

capillary refill test 110–11

carrying weights 115–16
catching the horse
   difficult 51–2
   from the field 13
chaff 73
clothing
   for examination 123, *124*
   for horse 92–102
   for working with horses 18, *20*, 21,
      113–14, 124, *125*
coarse mixes 73, *74*, 75, *76*, 78
colour of horse 5–12
concentrates 75–8
coolers 99
country code 117–18
crib biting 54
cubes, feed 73, *74*, 75, 78
curry comb *25*, *26*, 27

deep litter 35
digestion 68–70
domesticated horse 46–51
droppings 64–6, 109
   removal from pasture 66

electric fencing 63

examination
  clothing 123–4, *125*
  location 123
  performance 126

farrier *104*, 106
feed
  daily ration 73, *74*, 75, 79
  quality 68
  requirements 69–70, 73, 75
  types 70–3
feeding 68–70
  and exercise 68–9
  frequency 68, 75
fencing 60–3
fillet string 97, 98
fire precautions 117
first aid 118–20
flight instinct 46, 47
flooring 36-7
foot
  picking up 16, *17*, 22
  structure 103, *105*

gates 63
  leading through 14–15
gender 1
girth 80–2, 88–9
grooming 28–30
  kit 24–8, 31
  method 31–4
  reasons for 24

hacking 55–8
  safety 117–18
  winter conditions 116

handling the horse 16–17
  in stable 55
hard hat 113–14
hay
  meadow 71
  quality 70–1
  rations 73–4, 79
  seed 71
  soaking 71
  threshed 71
haylage 72
haynet *75*
  safety 115
head collar
  catching horse 13, 14, 52
  grooming 29
  tacking up 82
health
  signs 109–11
  unwell horse 111–12
hearing sense 46–7, 54
hedges 62–3
height of horse 1–2
herd instinct 46, 52
hoof pick 22, 24, *25*, 108
horse at grass 60–7
  behaviour 48–51
  catching 13–15, 51–2
  daily checks 66–7
  fencing 60–4
  rugs 67, 95
  shelter 64–7
  water 63–4, 116

injury from tack 89–90

jogging 57–8

leading the horse 14, 18–21, 23
lifestyle of horse 46–8
lifting weights 115

maize 72
mane comb *25*, 27
markings 2, *3*, 4–5
martingales 84
    fitting 86–7
muck heap 41–3
mucking out 37–9, 40–1, 43–4
    complete 35, 40–1
    deep litter 35
    procedure 37–8, 40–1
    shavings 41
    tools *38*

napping 56–7
natural instincts 46–8
New Zealand rug 95
numnah 80

oats 70, 72, *74*, *76*

paper bedding 36
pasture management 64–6
points of horse *xi*, 1, 12
poisonous plants 66, 70
post and rail fencing 61
post and wire fencing 61–2
pulse rate 110, 111

ragwort in hay 70
respiration rate 110, 111

riding out 56–8
    safety 117–18
    winter conditions 116
roads
    accidents 120
    riding on 118
rolling 48
rubber flooring 36–7
rugging up 92, 93–5
rugs 92–9
    at grass 67, 95
    cleaning 98
    fitting 96–9
    New Zealand 95
    removing 96
    underblankets *93*, 95
saddle
    fitting 84–5
    points of *81*
    safety checks 89–91
    tacking up 80–2
safety
    riding 118
    tack 88–9
    yard 114–17
shavings bed 36
shelter at grass 64
shoeing, need for 103–6
shying 56
sight of horse 46–7
skin recoil test 109
skipping out 40, 41, 44, 45
slip knot *15*, 16
spooking 56
stable rubber 27
stabled horse 52–5

turning out 16, 21, 50–1
winter conditions 116
stabling, barn systems 54
standing horse up 18–19
stock fencing 63
straw bedding 35–6
sugar beet 72–3, *74, 77*
surcingle 94, 96, *97, 99*
sweat scraper *25, 27, 28*
sweat sheet 99

tack
cleaning 87–8
fitting 84–7, 91
injuries from 89–91
safety checking *88–9*
tacking up 80–4, 91
tail
bandaging 99–102
grooming 29, *30*, 32
temperament
feeding 70
stabling 54–5
temperature 109, 111

tetanus 113
trotting in hand 20
turning out 21–2
tying up 15–16, 18, 28

vices, stable 54
voice leading horse 19, 23

water supply 63–4, 116
watering 68–70
after work 69
horse at grass 63–4, 116
weaving 54
weeds 66
Weil's disease 113
wheelbarrow *38, 39*, 40, 43
wind sucking 54
worms, pasture management 65–6

yard safety
fire precautions 117
tidiness 114–15
winter conditions 116–17